I0002122

LORD GANESHA'S LAPTOP

Building a Radically Adaptive IT Organization in India: An Expat's Story

Vladi Ruppo

Copyright © 2020 Zalman (Vladimir) Ruppo

All rights reserved

The characters and events portrayed in this book are fictitious.
Any similarity to real persons, living or dead, is coincidental and
not intended by the author.

No part of this book may be reproduced, or stored in a retrieval
system, or transmitted in any form or by any means, electronic,
mechanical, photocopying, recording, or otherwise, without
express written permission of the publisher.

ISBN-13: 9798556387997
ASIN: B08M8YWF5R

To my fellow passengers of LH754 Frankfurt-Bangalore flights and to all other perpetual travellers, with love.

The soft overcomes the hard;
the gentle overcomes the rigid.
Everyone knows this is true,
but few can put it into practice.

LAOZI, TAO TE CHING

CONTENTS

Acknowledgments

First, many thanks to my wonderful and strange Ruppo family for accepting and forgiving my escape to India. Or at least for pretending to.

Sveta Guralnik was my supportive friend and partner during my years in Bangalore. An awesome writer and a scholar of Buddhism, Sveta guided me with her advice. And even more so, with her example of a stunning personal transformation.

Ulyana Shmid helped me crystallize the key ideas of this book. Without her meticulous attention to detail, clarity of thought, and deep understanding of the IT management issues, I would have struggled with my writing blocks forever.

The first book and its author are more demanding than toddlers. I have tested the infinite patience of my friends and family by sending them draft after draft. Gabi Lanyi, Shmuel Ruppo, Etienne Roux, Rashma Raveendra, Irina Ruppo-Malone, Santosh Godbole, Julia Kleyman, and others bravely read them and encouraged me every time I was ready to give up.

Special thanks to Natan Nasekin and Veronica Lasovsky, a wonderful translator from Russian, for making my "charming," Indo-Russian-Israeli-Leviathanian English a bit more civilized and conventional. And to Sushobhan Sen, for his thorough comments and remarks.

I would also like to express my deepest gratitude to all my former colleagues (and especially to those from India), for our intellectual adventures, professional discoveries, and the pure joy of working together. I am sure they see this story differently — "there are no facts only interpretations," as Nietzsche puts it. Still I hope they don't judge my interpretation too harshly.

My wonderful Israeli ex-boss (code-named "Yossi" in the book) used to say, "Don't confuse me with facts." To make my story less confusing, I've omitted a few details and fictionalised others. I've also changed all the names in the book, except my own — I accept responsibility both as an author and a character.

INTRODUCTION: LORD GANESHA AND THIS BOOK

Many years ago, I came to Bangalore from Jerusalem to set up a development centre of a British technology company. It was my first trip to India. Looking for gifts for my family in a stuffy cluttered souvenir shop on Commercial street, I found a small figurine of Lord Ganesha. Something was strange about it; I took a closer look. So colourful, full of life, opulent in his half-human half-elephant form, this ancient god of infinite wisdom was... casually working on his laptop.

A god with a laptop sounds like blasphemy in the West. What is he doing? Writing code? Passing time on Facebook? Sending emails to subordinates and devotees?

To find my answers, I had to live in India for the next 18 years, fly about 4.6 million miles with Lufthansa, and write this book. It has multiple facets, some hidden inside others, like Russian matryoshka dolls.

This is a story of a bumpy corporate journey — from software engineer to VP and general manager of a development centre that I founded and expanded to almost 2,500 employees.

And a tale of a personal change, from denial — to understanding, to acceptance, to love of my new home – India.

DEVELOPERS AND GODDESSES

Book I

PART I. LAPTOP IN THE CANDLELIGHT

Take-off

The "Fasten your seatbelts" sign is still on; the monotonous humming of announcements in three languages — German, English, and Hindi — is thankfully ending. I know these instructions by heart.

I am in a window seat, 81K, on the LH754 Frankfurt-Bangalore flight, in that sweet hump at the very top of a Boeing 747-8. Quoting Wikipedia, "... a habitat is the type of natural environment in which a particular species of organism lives. A species' habitat is those places where it can find food, shelter, protection and mates for reproduction."

Except for "mates for reproduction," this definition perfectly fits — LH754 is my habitat.

In the good old days, the upper deck hosted the first-class paradise, where fountains of Calvados and Dom Perignon gushed among gardens of caviar, lobsters, and fried pigeons. Then Lufthansa had to expand its business class to the upper deck, as there were more and more corporate travellers to Bangalore: neither first-class nobility nor economy-class sardines. It was mostly IT managers and experts; "people in software," as they are now called.

I'm one of them. There is nothing special about me. Like everyone else, I am in a mid-life crisis since early childhood. The only difference is, most of my fellow passengers are flying to India for a short business trip, while I am returning home.

Wait. Home?

Yeah, I live in India. No, I am not learning levitation or meditation in an ashram; I just work in high-tech. Boring.

Even after so many years in India, I remain a foreigner. A perpetual alien, a citizen of Lufthansa. There are only two ways to get Indian citizenship: to be born to Indian parents or to marry an Indian. So far, I've missed both opportunities.

Still, I am not worried about my identity. It's simple: I am a Russian-Israeli who runs the Indian branch of the British company, MCR Ltd — a world leader in the digital television domain, owned by an Australian tycoon. The company is managed by our brilliant CEO, Ron — a Romanian American Israeli living in London.

I'm flying home after a corporate meeting at our London headquarters. I met Ron there, and he confirmed his visit to India in a couple weeks. Our boss looks like a perfectly shaven Santa Claus, hiding his natural kindness behind a sarcastic chuckle. Looks are deceptive: Ron is a steel fist in a silk glove, as shrewd and wise, as two King Solomons. He enjoys his witticisms as much as he likes parties and ridiculously expensive wine. Ron flies exclusively first class so that we, mere MCR mortals, can fly business class, looking down on fellow mortals in economy. The latter have no one to look down on, except the ground-dwellers far below.

When in India, Ron is going to make a call on the future of a platform, Evo (a short for Evolution), which I am in charge of. If Evo is terminated, I will have to look for another job. How do I convince Ron that Evo deserves to live on? And that I should continue working in India?

Ron appreciates good stories. I have eight hours and twenty minutes of flight time to think of a story to tell him.

The plane is taxiing to the runway.

How did it all start, anyway?

The Knight and the Pawn

My relatives have a nasty habit of dying of cancer. Many years ago, when my brother passed away, I decided to radically change course. So I left my first software startup in Jerusalem to spend a couple of fabulous years at the Hebrew University, studying philosophy and comparative religion.

I enjoyed studying, but it was more about learning historical "facts" rather than getting deep insights into the nature of reality. The academic world turned out to be no closer to heaven than the corporate one; they played the same games by similar rules. Once I figured them out, I received an invitation to a Ph.D. program in the United States.

By then, I had run out of cash. For some odd reason, comparative religion scholars get paid less than software developers. Could it be that software development decodes the meaning of life better than the history of religions?

This is how I ended up in the Jerusalem branch of MCR, among inspired professionals. Our team developed a cutting-edge system for transmitting data over satellites. I enjoyed writing viciously sophisticated C++ code and spending nights in search of the most elegant design patterns. Still, our work went for a toss, as they say in India: due to management blunders, we released a perfectly engineered piece of software space junk.

I felt enough was enough; to become a master of my own destiny, I decided to move up as a manager.

It wasn't an easy call for me. Born and brought up in Soviet Russia, I shared its common disdain for sales, management, and other "useless" professions. I used to think that a proper job brings tangible (or at least emotional) value, like the job of a doctor, a scientist, or a writer.

Well, if not a writer, then a software developer: writing code is a type of creative writing. Developers create new worlds out of nothing using the words of programming languages, almost like the biblical God creating our world with his Word. Managers, I felt, claimed ownership of the work of real creators — engineers.

An ancient Gnostic myth tells a similar story: a benevolent creator of our world is a radical introvert. Evil angels-managers proclaim that they are the creators. The true creator does not care about the usurpers — he is too busy developing version 2.0 of our Universe.

Not to depend on managers, it made sense to become a manager myself, the higher in the hierarchical pyramid, the better. I found myself in good company — most of my seven hundred colleagues in the Israeli MCR had similar aspirations. Jogging in a crowd is not my sport of choice, so I decided to move like a daring chess knight, rather than a persistent corporate pawn.

The MCR business grew by leaps and bounds, and we looked for developers all around the world. I prepared an exquisitely slick presentation, as beautiful as the Mona Lisa or my C++ code, to convince Ron, our CEO, that St. Petersburg, Russia, was the best place to find excellent developers at a cost much lower than in Europe.

By sheer coincidence, I had been born, brought up, and then graduated in computer sciences in St. Petersburg.

Convincing Ron was easier than I thought — he was curious about people, he loved geo-diversity, and he was always ready to throw a few bucks around and see what stuck. I'd gotten Ron's royal nod of approval for relocating to St. Petersburg and opening up a development centre there. He approved recruiting twenty engineers to develop interactive TV apps, as demand in this domain was expected to surge.

This is how I liked to tell my story: I had crammed my travel bags with stuff for a gloomy, slushy, and depressing Dostoyevskian winter in St. Petersburg. But karma had another plan. Instead of booking a flight to Russia, our travel department made a minor mistake. They booked me to Bangalore, India.

The knight is the only chess piece that can "fly above" the chessboard. But it can't fly straight. Likewise, my leap over people's heads landed at an unexpected destination.

Stunned, I stepped out of the plane, all wrapped up in my "shuba" fur coat, "ushanka" fur hat, and "valenki" felt boots — and found myself in the Indian swelter, instead of the dreary, cold Russian winter!

I had told this story so many times that I was beginning to believe it myself.

Welcome to Bangalore

Bangalore is dubbed a Garden city; a formerly sleepy town for retired government employees with a good climate — not too hot in the summer (below 35° Celsius), not too cold in the winter (above 15° Celsius).

Thanks to favourable legislation and climate, Bangalore has exploded, losing its gardens and its old charm, and reaching more extreme temperatures as a result of deforestation. But it has reinvented itself as the software capital of India, with a population of about ten million people, give or take a few million. At least a million people are working in the IT and IT-enabled services sector. Almost every tech company has a presence here.

Wishing to say something nice about the city, locals often mention that Bangalore has the largest number of pubs in Asia. However, this amazing fact is only known in Bangalore.

The city has been renamed Bengaluru — its authentic pre-British name. It is still Bangalore to me.

My first day in Bangalore was marked by utter disarray and panic. I stepped out of my posh, drowning-in-greenery hotel for a walk, to deliberately lose myself in the city. That's what I always do in new cities — I look for something unexpected.

In Bangalore, everything was unexpected.

India was so densely populated — with humans, animals, and deities — it was overwhelming. Dirty streets with dilapidated sidewalks were swarming with people. Alongside roads, skinny cows were chewing newspapers, looking sad and detached. Bright, colourful figurines with the mysterious smiles of Indian movie stars queued on temple walls and roofs. They say there are three hundred and thirty million gods in India; no wonder the lines were so long.

Colours, sounds, and smells — everything was off the chart, stunning, shocking. Our customary European ideas of "beautiful" and "ugly" were meaningless here. This was a different world.

I was dizzied by Bangalore crowds, traffic, and the cacophony of honking. A request "Horn OK Please" was painted on the wide orange buttocks of Indian lorries. At the entrance to an Indian temple, I was told to ring a bell so that God could notice me. Here in noisy and colourful India to make your presence known, one must be loud.

"India is all about extremes. There is too much of everything, and everything is too much for a European," I was thinking. "India is not for the faint of heart."

As the Tao Te Ching — my favourite book of ancient Chinese wisdom — puts it,

Five colours blind the eye.

Five notes deafen the ear.

Five flavors make the palate go stale.

Too much activity deranges the mind.

My initial relocation agreement was for six months. I didn't plan to prolong it.

Recruitment: First Catch

Bangalore had felt a bit cosier when I got some help from our sister company — they kindly offered me a place in their basement office near the Ulsoor lake.

The office was minimalistic, to put it mildly; there was no basic infrastructure, no furniture, "no nothing," as they say. Instead, there was a sweetish, mouldy smell of decay and a wonderful startup garage feeling: the poorer the environment, the bigger the dreams. There was no UPS or generator backup, so every time power went down, we lit up candles and kept working on our laptops in the flickering light. "Laptops in the candlelight" sounds so romantic. It's almost a metaphor for India.

Our sister company helped me find my first candidates. The night we published our first recruitment ad in the *Times of India*, I went to bed early, in anxious anticipation of my morning catch.

As has often happened to me in India, I got much more than I expected. Our modest email server crashed under the flow of resumes. There were no big fish in my net — almost all five thousand emails were from "freshers" (fresh college graduates). Taking no chances, they sent multiple copies of their resumes. "To be noticed in a crowd in India, you honk loudly on the roads, ring the temple bells, and send your resume five times in a row," I thought.

These resumes were longer than James Joyce novels, and even more boring, as they proudly mentioned every minor detail: "I have four and a half months of experience in...." I was glad they did not mention days and minutes.

I interviewed a bunch of the candidates; none were any good. There were more than ten thousand engineering colleges in India, churning out more than a million graduates every year. I read that up to seventy-five percent of Indian freshers were unemployable. I felt I got emails from most of them.

The head of HR from our sister company shared his own experience with freshers:

He had twenty interviews lined up. The first candidate surprised him with an authentic answer to the question about his weaknesses, "Sir, I can't focus on my job when I am hungry, Sir!"

The head of HR liked the answer. He then asked other candidates the same question — and heard the same reply nineteen more times. He still didn't know if the first fresher had shared his experience with others, or if the college had done such a good job preparing always hungry graduates for an interview.

Advertising didn't work for me — I didn't have the patience to sort through the thousands of duplicate resumes and interview hundreds of random candidates. So I started working with third-party recruitment consultants. I had to explain to them that I didn't care much about years of experience, like others in India, as experience was no proof of capability for me. Instead, I was looking for engineers who could have fit in with my team at MCR Israel: sharp, sceptical, and creative. And, of course, adjusted to the local culture.

Apropos local culture, I had to figure it out somehow...

Patterns of India

The way people live impacts the way they write (and ruin!) their software. To work better with my first Indian "resources" (as we dub engineers with "charming" corporate indifference), I had to understand their realities and to feel the heartbeat of their country.

There are several good ways to do that — you could socialize with locals, work together, or have a romantic relationship. I was keen on trying it all, but the quickest way to learn something about a country was by... reading local newspapers. That's why I'd become a loyal subscriber of the Deccan Herald.

I read Indian newspapers inside out: the front page, full of stories on cricket, politics, and other important matters, usually left me uninterested. Inner page headlines were eye-openers:

"Human Sacrifice Case Lodged,"

"Village Elders Council Sentenced a Girl to Gang-Rape,"

"Seven Lawyers Killed in a Road Accident," and more.

The very fact that these items had not made it to the front page, apparently since they were too trivial and ordinary by the local standards, spoke volumes.

I was looking for patterns, but India appeared too diverse, extreme, and multidimensional. It was only exceptions, without rules. How do you combine forty-five million rural households without electricity — and spaceflight? Gandhi's life of service to humanity and nonviolence — and violent riots, honour killings, and acid attacks on wives? My first conclusion was, "India defies patterns. It is malleable, mouldable, combining opposites and extremes. Its citizens can adapt to any way of life, any language, religion, and pattern. India is so diverse that everything you say about India is true and false at the same time." Including this very statement, as I realized later.

I couldn't make sense of it just by reading newspapers in the comfort of my air-conditioned room. To understand my developers better, I had to feel the soil they had grown from. I started going out of town every weekend.

MCR had a generous relocation policy, providing me with a big, comfy Innova van. Given the mad chaos of Indian roads, there was no way I would drive myself. Rajesh, my new driver from the state of Tamil Nadu, was as adventurous and resourceful as Indiana Jones.

I doubt that the tough American hero would be half as efficient as Rajesh, helping me jump the endless and irate queue to a temple, pacifying angry villagers after accidentally running over their favourite chicken, or simply dealing with clerks, policemen, and customs officers. Rajesh did everything with ease.

Very tense on Indian roads initially, soon I came to trust Rajesh's art of driving. I also trusted the triple protection on top of our car's dashboard: Lord Ganesha's statue joined forces with the Jewish Tefilat Haderech (the prayer for a safe journey) that I brought on Rajesh's request from Israel, and a gold plated magnet with a quote from the Gospel of John, gifted by Rajesh's mother, who was newly converted to Christianity. Every time I looked at the dashboard, I was reassured by this trio of divine supporters — a rare example of interfaith cooperation and teamwork. I assumed that cheerful and opulent Lord Ganesha was the team leader. Rajesh, reverent to all religions as most Indians, used to decorate Ganesha's figurine with a garland of white jasmine flowers every Monday. "You won't get far on Indian roads without divine intervention," I thought.

After every weekend trip, I returned to our basement office near Ulsoor Lake, filled to the brim with experiences of the magical and serene Indian countryside. It was like a parallel universe to the noisy Bangalore hive.

After visiting about a dozen out of twenty-nine Indian states, I had to acknowledge that some of them were no more similar to each other than Spain to Norway. Not just states — every town or village in India had its unique centuries-old traditions, impacting its native software engineers in its unique ways.

Each religion shapes its followers in its unique ways, too; Hindus, Muslims, and Christians, as well as Jains and Sikhs, were among our first employees — and they worked really well together.

The languages we speak impact the way we think. "As many languages you know, as many times you are a human being." Everyone around me was a human being at least four- or five-fold.

Translating from English

In the meantime, I was hiring my first engineers — interactive app developers and testers. No one had heard of MCR in Bangalore, we had no brand name or reputation. But I was a local curiosity of sorts, like a two-headed snake, or a white monkey. Or even like a low-key movie star: strangers in the streets sometimes asked me for a photo together. Reporting to a foreigner in India was prestigious; so I, myself, was the recruitment bait, and managed to catch a few risk takers.

First visits from other MCR sites to India were made. The first bottles of Kingfisher beer were drunk, first corporate fights were fought, and first projects got delivered.

I thought we had done a good job. But without quality or performance metrics in place, "good" or "bad" was totally subjective. We got thanked sometimes, blamed more often. I stood up for my developers and testers as best I could. I was building bridges and translating from Indian English to Israeli English and British English.

How do you explain to Indian engineers that "bloody Indians" coming from our London colleague was an expression of admiration, not an expletive? How do you explain to Israelis that "we are doing everything we can to make the release on time" coming from our Indian engineers meant they were late?

My timid Indian developers were happy to outsource all corporate fights with the West to me. From my Western colleagues I kept hearing that my people made unrealistic promises, that the quality of their

work was low. They expected overly detailed speci-
fications, their communication skills were poor, and
so on.

I fought back, explained, and argued — but in my
heart of hearts, I could see their point. The issues
were real, and it seemed like most of them had a common denominator.

And, indeed, during my trip to Mysore, I discovered
this root of all evil.

Root of Evil

One Sunday, Rajesh and I went to the Mysore Palace.
The queue to the palace was as long as a nightmare.
Bored to death, I was watching the sophisticated
workflow of admitting visitors: one skinny clerk sold
tickets at the entrance, another one, right next to
him, checked them. A third clerk, two meters away,
checked the same tickets again and finally granted the
"right of passage" inside.

There was no way to cut the line, so I indulged in
idle reflections. "What an inefficiency," I was ponder-
ing. "The simplest task in India is an excuse to hire as
many people as possible."

Dozens of bored men in bath slippers, dirty shirts, and
dhoti — traditional skirts or rather loincloths — are
swarming at every checkpoint. They are so busy raising and lowering the barrier — all together!

"Office boys," often no longer young, clean offices and run errands. "Lift boys" — elevator operators — sit in an elevator for ten hours a day pushing the floor buttons.

Timidly smiling janitors in public bathrooms are eagerly waiting for a visitor to ask them for paper towels or toilet paper, grateful for any request — and for a few rupees. Most families have "maids" (housekeepers), drivers, and cooks. Managing them is sometimes more difficult than cooking a meal or cleaning an apartment by yourself. Still, giving a job to as many people as possible is the most humane tradition.

In an overpopulated country, a job is more than a job. It distinguishes a person from the faceless, jobless crowd, and defines one's identification and value. I am important, as I am a Bureaucrat, a Lorry Driver, an Assistant Door Opener, a General Manager, or a Junior Button Pusher.

"I work, therefore I exist."

An overabundance of workforce leads to the devaluation of the individual. Did someone go missing? Meet with an accident? Get carried away by an evil spirit? Not to worry — millions of people can't wait to take his place. Preference is given to relatives: in government institutions, the position of the deceased is inherited by default by his widow or son.

What is it, absolute redundancy and inefficiency? Or

a pragmatic, compassionate approach that allows the family to survive the loss of the breadwinner? Probably both at the same time. Absurd? No, the merciful economics of overpopulation.

That is what was going through my mind as I inched closer to the entrance. Then I heard a mighty, rageful growl, descending from above. This must be how a male walrus roars when it sees a rival during mating season. Yet it was neither a walrus, nor a lion, nor His Majesty Maharaja of Mysore. It was the senior bureaucrat, "babu," a manager of the ticket sales office. Sprawling in his chair, he growled lazily and ominously at his scrawny, trembling crew. I watched him with silent awe, wondering if this "Manager Sir" got his job due to his innate facial expression of contempt for mortals, or if it had developed over years of selfless service.

In private life, maybe he was an exemplary husband and father. But to me, exhausted by the heat and the endless queue, this burly ruler of a teeny-tiny world appeared as the embodiment of a cosmic hierarchy. He was the root of all managerial evil — an archetype of the command-and-control style that I hated so much.

Social patterns are contagious. Engineers breathed the same air as this babu bureaucrat and millions of his brethren — and contracted the same viruses. Software managers brought up in a culture of redundancy and hierarchy, with maids, cooks, and guards at home, naturally handed over second-rate work to subordinates and pushed them around. Their obedient "resources" — JavaScript proletarians and testing peasants — seldom asked themselves, "Why do we do what we do?" They already knew the answer: "Because our boss told us to!"

The outdated management culture inherited from the British colonial system had long since died out in the metropolis, but it had persisted and evolved in the natural reserves of Indian government institutions. From these musty and stuffy bureaucratic thickets, command-and-control hierarchical management was spreading through the brand-new offices of IT companies, poisoning the developers' minds.

As I was leaving the palace, yet another clerk stopped me to check my ticket for the fifth time. Recklessly indifferent to papers, I had thrown it in the dustbin in the very first hall. I would have remained in the palace forever, as one of its most valuable exhibits, had Rajesh the driver not come to my rescue.

Sir Vladi

On a sultry evening, after visiting the palace, Rajesh and I went to a small festival near Mysore. India uses its very own units of numbering: lakhs (one hundred thousand) and crores (ten million). Even one lakh was too much for me: in the stifling crowd, I felt like a mouldy morsel of cheese drowning in a huge lake of hot spicy chocolate. Rajesh managed to drag me to the coolness of the air-conditioned car. In gratitude for saving my life, I granted him the priceless privilege of calling me "sir."

At first, it had been hard for me to accept the Indian tradition of addressing seniors as "sir" or "ma'am." It was along a vector of hierarchy alien to me. From day one, I had demanded that Rajesh call me by my first name, without any "sir." But no matter how hard he tried, he just couldn't get over years of upbringing and custom. I started calling him "sir" in retaliation. Rajesh flinched every time, as if from a mild electric shock. By demanding equality, I had been tormenting my driver. Only when he — twice in a day! — saved me, I gave in.

A driver may do what the engineers may not — after all, we were a Western company, not the Mysore Palace. Rajesh was the only one in the office who could call me "Vladi, sir." And he was very proud of his privilege.

The day after my trip to Mysore, I had a chat with Nidhi, our web developer. She had just returned from a business trip to the UK. This was Nidhi's first trip abroad, so I expected to hear words of admiration for good old England in exchange for my complaints about the Mysore crowds and the heat.

Nidhi struggled to be polite. "England is not too bad, actually... It's clean... Houses, trees, roads — everything is like in India only. But it was so cold. And there were so few people — no energy. It was boring. I really missed people, Vladi... I was so homesick!"

To each their own.

Bangalore Choir

Once I received an email from an Israeli project manager:

Subject: Poor programming skills

Vladi, we were expecting a release from your team last Friday. No one bothered to inform us about the delay. When we've finally received the code, it turned out the merge was done sloppily!

I would ask you to discuss this incident with the team, as it reflects their poor understanding of the code structure and inattention to my requirements.

Since I can't rely on your people, I'll have to find other resources to complete my project.

Best regards,

David

Oh, darn. I was counting on this project so much! I called the manager of the team working for David on the carpet.

"Vladi, I'm sorry, but David's people sent us the wrong

instructions for the merge... Besides, David has delayed our training for the last three months. Means,
without training we have to guess..."

"Okay. But why didn't you inform them of the delay
on Thursday?"

"We wrote to them... perhaps they didn't notice...."

I was pretty annoyed with David, but I could relate
to him. When something is wrong, Western engineers
send an email written in large, bold, red font, capital letters. My Indian engineers hide their problems
deep inside their polite, mile-long scrolls written in
formal Victorian English, in small print. No wonder
David didn't notice the message about a delay.

"But how come you didn't tell ME anything, huh?"

I was getting more and more irritated.

"Sorry, we didn't want to bother you, sir... I mean,
Vladi."

I've heard a story about a Western tourist waiting for
a bus somewhere in India.

> He asks the locals when the bus would arrive.
> He is told, "Very soon, sir!" After half an hour
> of waiting, the foreigner asks again — the an-
> swer is the same. The same repeats again, an
> hour later. Finally, a passerby tells him, "Sir, the
> buses don't stop here anymore!"
>
> "But why didn't they tell me before?" yells the
> tourist.

"Well, they didn't want to upset you, sir!" the passerby replies.

Likewise, my managers agreed to unrealistic deadlines, not to have to say "no" to our internal customers. Like the husband of an adulterous wife in Russian jokes, I was the last one to get the bad news. My people wanted their boss to be happy. A happy boss doesn't have to do anything, just praise occasionally, and growl, like that walrus-like babu. Telling a boss about problems is doubly wrong. First, it upsets the boss. Second, it reveals subordinates' incompetence, as they couldn't fix the issue by themselves.

No matter how many times I tried to change this pattern, nothing changed. It was reinforced in family, in school, in college, and at every encounter with government clerks.

Yossi, my imposing and friendly Israeli boss, wanted to help my young team. When he arrived in Bangalore, he gathered our engineers and made them chant "NO!" in unison so that they would learn that you can and should argue with your superiors!

For fifteen minutes, Yossi conducted the orchestra of the shyly giggling developers, bleating "nooooo" in many voices. No one — not even me — told him: "NO, Yossi! Stop this insanity, please!"

And it's good I didn't: Yossi, our friend, left, happy with his success, and gave us extra money for communication training.

Hodja Nasruddin as a Management Guru

Hiring engineers to work on interactive TV apps, I was dreaming of developing generic infrastructure and eventually taking over the entire domain: "First we take Manhattan, then we take Berlin," as Leonard Cohen taught me.

But both my karma and my management had other plans. By the time we had hired a few engineers the market had changed. Expected surge in demand had not happened, so the company decided to stop development in this area.

That was painful and unexpected — what should my engineers do now?

To keep in shape, they tasked themselves with improving our sister company's website for free. And I started traveling between main MCR centres in Israel, the UK, and France, like a Buddhist monk with his begging bowl, trying to find some work for us through my old connections. I thought it would be a piece of cake. MCR were hiring left, right, and centre, so why not in India, at a much lower cost, right?

Wrong! I was so wet behind the ears. Middle managers who owned development work were in no hurry to share it with India. They were not accountable for the cost of development, so it was easier for them to hire locally, even at a higher price. MCR was not short of cash, so costs were not a big deal.

Ron, our CEO, benevolently watched these efforts from his celestial heights, curious if we would prove ourselves or just die quietly. He even helped me by putting a little pressure on a few managers. Then, without any apples dropping on me, I discovered Newton's Third Corporate Law: for every action in an organization, there is an equal and opposite reaction. The more pressure we applied to move projects to Bangalore, the more resistance we encountered. Engineers at MCR UK and MCR Israel started talking about secret plans to "Bangalore" them — move their jobs to India. This was utter rubbish; MCR was hiring everywhere. Yet perceptions matter more than reality.

Looking for medicine for this corporate paranoia, I had a sudden flashback. In childhood, I read a story about Hodja Nasruddin, a witty Sufi folklore hero and a popular character in Soviet-era children's literature. Once Hodja Nasruddin saw a tax collector drowning in the river. "Give me your hand!" Nasruddin shouted, trying to save him.

The man did not respond. Nasruddin kept shouting, but the half-drowned man didn't want to extend his hand.

Then wise Nasruddin figured it out. "Take my hand!!" he yelled.

The tax collector immediately grabbed his hand and was rescued.

Instead of asking overseas managers to give work to India, I offered to give them a hand, "It is easier to recruit in India! We will extend your team with people in Bangalore!"

Children's books give the best management advice. Changing the narrative helped beyond expectations. When foreign managers couldn't find people locally, they were willing to try us out. By the end of my second year, we expanded to about forty people (mostly in testing and Web technologies, but we also added a few Java and C++ developers) — doubling my initial quota.

The basement office had become too small for us. Together with our Indian sister company, we had moved to a brand-new building in the very centre of Bangalore.

Our new office was large and comfortable. There even was a separate management bathroom, as it was not appropriate for top management in India to mix with subordinates for such sensitive activities.

In every office in India, there are "office boys" and "cleaning ladies." Office boys serve tea to managers and visitors, do some cleaning, and run errands. Our first office boy's name was Stalin. No, he wasn't an offspring of Joseph Stalin as I had initially suspected. "Lenin" and "Stalin" are popular first names in Indian communist families. There is even an annual all-India congress, where hundreds of moustachioed Lenins gather. I was hoping to get an invite as Lenin's namesake, and started working on a fiery speech.

I was happy to extend my relocation agreement with MCR: how on earth could I leave the place where none other than Stalin served me masala tea twice a day! My Russian-speaking friends were dying of envy.

Wastebusket or Sailing Ship?

Meanwhile, there was nothing to be envious of: I was in the twilight zone between euphoria and frustration. On the one hand, we, MCR India, had proven our right to exist. I already had about seventy "resources." I was promoted to Director. Getting some extra paise was sweet. I was traveling around India and saw things that made me wonder: where are you, *National Geographic*?

But on the other hand....

When I returned from my trips to the West and distributed my modest loot among my people, their happy smiles splashed like goldfish in my glass, aquarium-like office. But our treasure was someone else's trash: we were given third-rate work of second-hand freshness. Stuff like support, bug fixing, and manual testing.

Following Nasruddin's wise advice, I had lent my men

to Western teams. Still, the flow of work that poured into India, both in volume and quality, resembled Bangalore's sewage drains, not the Ganges.

"First prove yourself in action," our Western colleagues were telling us. I would have been happy to, but our wastebasket was never given the opportunity to prove itself as a beautiful sailing ship. And even if it were, it would be impossible to prove anything. Western managers were not interested in our success, so they only saw what they wanted to see: communication problems, quality issues, and the like. We were caught in their perceptions like a fly in amber.

I felt stuck both professionally and socially.

Fish Tank

Every morning, Rajesh the driver would pick me up from my apartment near Ulsoor Lake and take me to the office on Lavelle Road. I usually stayed there until midnight — there was nothing for me to do in the huge, empty apartment I had just rented.

I went back home on foot every night — I needed to clear my head. The traffic was quieting down by then, but the stray dogs, so friendly and timid during the day, grew more aggressive in the dark. I wasn't brave, I was just plain stupid; I didn't know then how dangerous their packs could be. The dogs never attacked me, though. Probably, I was too alien and too foreign, even as prey.

I was used to being an outsider. At least, I thought I was. A Jew in Soviet Russia and a Russian (and now an Indian) in Israel. But in emotional India, to be professional, you have to be social: work is based on personal relationships and friendships. Good Indian organizations are like extended families.

I was left out.

In the corporate world, they talk about a "glass ceiling" — an invisible barrier that doesn't let women or minorities advance in their careers. I was banging my head against a glass wall: the walls of my spacious aquarium office were transparent to emphasize my "open" and "transparent" management style. But these glass walls had become an invisible barrier between "them" and me — the border between the realms.

My "open door policy" didn't help much: no one entered my open door without an invitation. India honours seniority both by age and by corporate hierarchy. Foreigners are treated with respect. A foreigner, manager, and senior in years, I enjoyed triple respect — certainly, well deserved!

And, with it, complete alienation.

Paradise or Hell?

My engineers politely agreed with me about everything, but it did not excite me. As a typical Russian Israeli, I enjoyed a good argument. I simply couldn't communicate in this suffocatingly formal style.

"Please don't get up. This is an international company, not an Indian college!" I asked as I was passing by an engineer seated at his workstation. He was getting ready to stand at attention.

"Yes, sir!" The young man replied, rising from his chair, as he had done his entire life.

I had to stop and fix it.

"Don't call me 'sir,' please!"

"Of course… as you say, Sir Vladi, sir!"

My muffled roar, which I had learned from the Mysore Palace bureaucrat, frightened the dumbfounded guy even more.

When I first started working in Bangalore, I thought I had ascended to some managerial paradise: subordinates were angelically obedient, without that endless Israeli bickering! But after a few months, I realized that I had fallen into a special circle of hell reserved for foreign managers in India. Yes, the developers did what I asked — precisely what I asked, without questioning me, out of respect. How could I build the lean and mean organization of my dreams — informal, agile, and innovative — with "resources" as soft as dough?

Too bad I didn't make it to St. Petersburg!

I was dangerously close to leaving... but where could I go? I was not really welcome at MCR Jerusalem: a Cain's mark of "traitor" and an "enemy of the people" had been glowing on my forehead since the rumours about "Bangalored" employees began to spread.

Planet Mars seemed a much better option for my future career.

Agni Theyyam

While I was waiting for the first commercial flight to Mars, Rajesh the driver took me to Kerala on one of the long weekends.

As we crossed the state border, a sculpture of a hammer and sickle on an explicitly phallic pedestal suddenly appeared out of the darkness. Typical for Kerala, where the lingam is sacred, and the Communist Party is one of the main political forces. Welcome to the land of palm trees, mosques, tile roofs, gods, and communists.

Until the middle of the twentieth century, matriarchy reigned in some areas of Kerala: clans were ruled by women; property was passed from mother to daughter. A woman could have several husbands. One of them would stay overnight — unless the slippers of a nimbler contender were already sitting by the house door. The lucky husband had to go home to his mom in the morning. The children were raised by their mother's older brother.

This operating model of family life prevented the very possibility of fights or issues. Everyone was happy, including husbands — after all, mom's food is the best.

Alas, time is destructive, and the sun of matriarchy has set. Almost total literacy, combined with mass poverty, generates riotous political activity. Concerned about social justice, forty-odd million citizens of Kerala constantly organize strikes, walkouts, and rallies. This is not great for business, so many are forced to go elsewhere for work, including to Bangalore.

On the advice of Nidhi, our web engineer from Kerala, Rajesh the driver and I went to a remote village in the middle of banana, rubber tree, and spice plantations. We arrived about midnight. A three-meter-high fire was burning in the middle of the courtyard.

A few bare-chested musicians in dhoti loincloths drummed forcefully and absent-mindedly, standing beside the fire.

A young man in a corner of the courtyard was preparing to perform. He was wearing a bright wide skirt and a dark maroon, papier mâché apron, with a belly and massive female breasts. His face was painted in an Aztec-like black and red: brick cheeks in large patterns and huge purple lips. His dark eyes, the size of half his face, were circled, and the white pupils inside were rolling erratically.

Someone handed the young man a small bottle. I thought it was "feni" — the fermented cashew apple juice. Or perhaps "toddy" — palm juice fermented in the sun, tasting like a malt drink, and inebriating as champagne.

Looking closer, I noticed the label of cheap whiskey on the bottle.

After taking a sip, the young man looked at the mirror readily extended to him. He instructed an assistant to fix his huge silver fangs. Then he glanced again — and suddenly, a miracle of transformation occurred. A white flash of light cut through the darkness of his eyes. Looking at himself in the mirror, he recognized an ancient goddess. His eyes rolled back. There was nothing human left in him.

The half-naked drummers' beat got more and more demanding, subduing my heartbeat. The goddess's feet, encased in massive silver anklets, trembled impatiently. The last element of her attire had been arranged. It was a huge maroon painted circle, about two meters in diameter, all embroidered with shining patterns.

The goddess rose and walked through the crowd, dancing to the drum rumble and swinging her curved sword. Her graceful and threatening movements were precise and soulless. Then, suddenly, vibrating with excitement, she threw herself into the fire. Two men tried to pull her away, but she escaped. The flame lured her as a candle attracts a moth. Another leap into the fire... and another one....

After several leaps of the goddess into the heart of the flames, the fire was extinguished. A pile of red-hot coals was scattered around the courtyard. The goddess began a fierce ceremonial dance on a living carpet of flaming coals — barefoot!

Almost hypnotized by the elaborate drumming pattern, I fell into a sort of a trance myself. Alas, not a deep one: I was standing barefoot, like everyone else — the territory of Theyyam is sacred — and accidentally stepped on a coal. The sharp pain of the burn reminded me that it was all real — an unearthly figure flying heavily over a carpet of burning coals, the rhythm of drums spiralling upward into the hot, humid sky, and the tidal waves of the dark palm sea around the courtyard.

In about ten minutes, it was over; the coals were cooling. The goddess went up to the landlord who had ordered the ceremony — the Agni Theyyam — and blessed him, cawing menacingly and threatening someone invisible with her curved sword. Another young man was already getting ready to perform.

The goddess took off her attire and washed off the intricate pattern, and a skinny young man with the arrogant face of a brahmin intellectual emerged. I approached him in awe:

"Please excuse my curiosity, but aren't your feet burned? Don't you feel pain?"

The young man was respectful, calm, and friendly.

"No, sir. When the goddess enters me, I feel nothing."

"May I ask where you have learned this?"

"From my father, sir. And he learned it from his."

I left him my business card, asking him to invite me to the next ceremony. Unfortunately, this one was the last of the season. They performed Theyyam only for two winter months. The rest of the year, the "goddess" worked as an electrician.

I was smitten and discombobulated.

"Rajesh!"

"Sir?"

"Rajesh, what do you say? Wasn't it absolutely amazingly awesome?"

"Sir..."

"Have you ever seen anything like this?"

"No, sir, never."

Rajesh fell silent. However, silence didn't come easy to my Indiana Jones from Tamil Nadu:

"But, sir, when I was on a temple pilgrimage, even I walked on coals."

"You?! Where?"

"In Sabarimala temple only, also in Kerala. You need to fast for forty days, then God enters you — and you can walk on coals."

"Can we go there?"

"Sure, sir, we should! Only there are no roads. We will walk through the jungle... for two weeks only, sir!"

Rajesh's eyes lit up. He had already started planning a trip with his boss through the humid and hot jungle — a hell of paradise.

I was still shaking. The rhythm of the drums still pounded in my temples.

No, I was not in St. Petersburg. I was in a country where Stalin serves me tea. Where gods enter electricians and drivers — and God knows when they leave them. I decided I should be more cautious with the locals, just in case.

I told my silly story of the India ticket mishap every time I was asked what had brought me to India. But the truth was, I had no one to blame for my choice. An influential VP of Indian origin, whose office in our London headquarters had been next to Ron's, had long wanted to set up a shop in Bangalore. "In an internal competition between development centres, VP has some advantage over a software engineer like me," I thought — and opted to work for him in India.

But, in fact, I did arrive in Bangalore with my Russian

baggage. Not "valenki" or Dostoevsky, but my rigid vision of what we should be like and my aggressive command-and-control management style.

Of course, "fixing" India was easier than changing myself. Still, a piece of coal from Agni Theyyam burned a hole in my virtual felt boots. "No, I'm not going anywhere. If electricians in India can walk on burning coals, engineers can probably write awesome code. All I need to do is create the right conditions."

I only wish I knew how....

The Beauty of the Code and the Peppered Watermelon

I looked at the module design presented by the head of our Microsoft technology team and almost wept at how boring and ugly it was.

Software development is an art form. Beautiful code works better than ugly one. But what is "beautiful"? India likes extreme combinations of colours, smells, and tastes, totally unpalatable to a Westerner. My guys ate pickles with jam; they peppered and salted the watermelons we served in our pantry. If we couldn't agree on what was "yummy" and what was "yucky" — could we ever agree on the aesthetics of software?

Taking a deep breath, I asked if Shiri, the young Israeli

team leader who had asked for this work, had seen the document. If not, I'd still have time to correct it....

"I'm sorry," the engineer said, embarrassed, "but this is Shiri's document. The design is hers. All we have to do is to implement it in code."

This was the moment of truth. As an honest engineer, I had to call Shiri, tell her what I thought of her sickening design, and suggest a better alternative — mine. Only problem, after that, no one from Shiri's department would ever give us any work.

In a short but bloody battle between honesty and common sense, honesty lost. Work on the project continued successfully, without my advice.

This was not the only project where my overseas colleagues easily managed without my help. Considering themselves excellent engineers, they wanted to work directly with my people, without any help from me.

And then complained to me about them.

Alex, our programming guru from Jerusalem, whom I knew back in Russia, clearly explained why he was not transferring his work to India, "If I use your guys, they'll still be yours. I want to work with my own people, not yours!"

Browsing through the Tao Te Ching, I got an idea of what to do.

Eighty Pages of Wisdom

The Tao Te Ching? How was Chinese wisdom relevant in India?

Immersion into Indian philosophy takes a lifetime or even a few, but my Bangalore contract was just for six months, extended each time for another six months. "I don't have time for thick volumes of the Indian Gita and Upanishads!" I told myself. But the Tao Te Ching was a high-speed elevator. It was just about eighty pages, and here I was, at the top of the wisdom of the East, calmly contemplating the world below.

In the West, issues that cannot be solved by brute force are solved by even greater force and eloquence. But action only causes reaction. No one listens to managers' beautiful speeches, especially when they say the right things (the wrong ones at least wake up the bewildered subordinates). Even Ron, our almighty and omniscient CEO, couldn't convince his people to move work to India. They always found valid arguments, "Yes, Ron, but...."

Reading the Tao Te Ching helped me realize that if a manager has to "put pressure" and "convince" to get things done, then something is wrong in the organization.

I was in the East, and the East is on an eternal quest for harmony. Not obsessive efforts, but the calm, detached "non-doing" of Tao. A meta-action at a higher level — the opposite of both inaction and obsessive overwork.

Therefore the Master acts without doing anything

And teaches without saying anything

Everything happens around the Master as if by itself.

Instead of trying to get projects transferred by pushing, pressing, and begging, and then arguing about the outcomes, all I needed to do was exhale and create a flow. And to do it, I should....

Love and Organizational Structure

I should start with the organizational structure. Like an x-ray, the structure exposes the corporate skeleton in its dazzling and shameful nakedness, revealing the root causes of corporate maladies.

My engineers were organized into technology lines: Java, C/C++, web technologies, and testing. All the line managers, naturally, reported to me. I gained a lot from moving work to India. The growth in the number of subordinates lifted my career up like the influx of water in a river lock lifts a boat. But the transfer of work should benefit those who decide on the transfer! So the best thing I could do was step aside and not get in the way. Following Hodja Nasruddin's advice, "to give a helping hand" literally means to amputate that hand and hand it to those in need of help.

This was our first major "reorg": each of the centres in London, Jerusalem, and Paris had established their own "software colony" in Bangalore with full authority over deliveries. Engineers who had previously reported to me had become subordinates of our internal customers (aka foreign rulers). I had been left with ceremonial, "dotted line" reporting as a consolation.

I had always believed in fairies and unicorns, but this was the first time I witnessed a real miracle. The work flowed to us by itself, like water from a rock under the blow of a biblical Moses' rod. The overseas managers had acquired a stake in Bangalore's success. They wanted to expand, and it was both cheaper and easier for them to do so in India.

When we had removed the obstacles and created a slope, the flow strengthened. Not only the quantity but the quality of work improved. Even the ownership of some legacy software components moved to India. At this rate, we would become equal players in about three hundred years — but we were not in a hurry.

Earlier, Western colleagues wanted to share their insights with me — as bold as they were generic. "Indian engineers are like this." Or, even broader, "Indians are like that." Now real people with names and characters emerged from the heavy fog of stereotypes: "Sudhir is like this," or "Pavitra is like that."

My people remained the same, but the change of structure changed the attitude. They were not just accepted but shown some love. It is much easier to love your subordinate than your "neighbour" — a corporate competitor.

Every overseas manager was convinced that his or her team was a unique exception in the vast ocean of alleged Indian "mediocrity." "My Indians are better, as I am their leader!" I kept hearing. I agreed with each and every one of them. Sure, your people are the best!

But my ego screamed and throbbed like a tiny creature — a leprechaun or a kitten — squeezed in the palm of my hand. It could not accept that "Vladi's Indians" had become someone else's.

I knew that had the ego kept its reporting lines, there would have been no flow. And had there been a flow, it would have washed my ego away like a river washes away a dead tree trunk blocking its current. Yet deep down, I felt like a dethroned maharaja.

According to a common belief, management is the best occupation for a megalomaniac. To me, management turned out to be a humbling experience. I hope others are luckier and can command and control their subordinates to their heart's content.

A White Monkey with Pink Heels

The obvious is the most difficult thing to realize (this statement is so obvious, it is not easy to realize, either). Only after stepping on the burning coals of the Agni Theyyam could I see the trivial truth: my social isolation in India was of my own making.

How did my Indian engineers see me? To them, I was neurotically impatient. My Russian jokes misfired; my Israeli irony missed the point. When I ate spicy Indian food, I burned my mouth. If I drank tap water, I ended up in the hospital. Even crossing a road — a trivial task for any Indian cow — was almost impossible for me, so I hid behind the local pedestrians. But I was great at giving instructions, excellent at criticizing everything, and perfect at explaining to others how things should be done. And they cheerfully smiled back at me.

Rabbi Zusia, a Hasidic guru who lived in Poland in the 18th century, said, "When I die, God will not ask me why I was not Moses or King David. He will ask me why I haven't been myself — just Zusia." I was always "fixing" and trying to turn our Surendras and Suchitras into "proactive," "assertive," and "innovative" Johns and Rebeccas. Rather than trying to turn Bangalore into St. Petersburg, it was time for me to finally land in Bangalore.

One day, the whole office went for an outing to a shady, rocky riverbank overgrown with brushy thickets, a few hours from Bangalore. On the way, we sang songs and played games. When we arrived, we admired the river and the rocks for a while and then moved on to the main part — the modest feast. Some drank Scotch with coke, others vodka with coke, while vegetarians drank coke with coke. The majority of Indian vegetarians do not drink alcohol. Some even don't need to: vegetarians in my team got tipsy on fresh air, laughter, and coke.

At first, the young people looked warily at me. But when they saw me drinking and laughing, they relaxed and started a simple but lively game. In the Soviet schools, such games — forcefully pouring vodka into each other's mouths — were considered too childish by eighth grade.

I was talking with a quiet, shy young religious Muslim chap, a senior C language developer. Of course, he didn't drink alcohol. I suggested we go get coffee.

"No, thank you, I don't drink coffee."

"Maybe some tea?"

"No, Vladi, I can't," he said, his voice muffled and a little sad.

"But why not?"

The developer looked at me, surprised he had to explain the obvious, and uttered with a sigh:

"Coffee and tea... uhmm... excite. Means, arouse. And I'm not married yet...."

Quality of life would improve for many if he were right.

Smoking in India is an act of family disobedience — smoking in the presence of elders is indecent and disrespectful. Yet people felt so comfortable in my presence that they dared to smoke. In response, I dared to eat biryani with my hand, like everyone else. My shirt got liberally strewn with oily rice. Eating biryani with my fingers was as difficult as catching sardines with a pitchfork. I simply didn't have the skills.

Still, I was able to impress the audience with my superpower: like the "X-Men," I could change the colour of my face! However, only to intense scarlet, and only when I ate something very spicy. That is, any Indian food other than sweets.

As we were crossing a creek barefoot on our way back to the bus, I had to roll up my jeans. Nidhi, the web technologies team leader, looked at my feet and roared with laughter:

"Oh, Vladi, your feet are pink! I can't believe my eyes! Look, people, he has such little pink heels!"

Nidhi, who looked like an ancient goddess oozing chthonic powers, couldn't stop laughing. Waves of mirth rocked and shook her voluminous body. It was this divine laughter that shattered my invisible shell.

One of the testers, who won the vodka game, said thoughtfully, admiring my heels, "Vladi, we thought you were like a big white monkey in your glass cage. But you're alright!"

And he threw up.

My young engineers acted naively, childishly, by European standards. But it was fun and easy for everyone. It was as if the local Adam and Eve didn't eat the apple but stayed happily in this luscious palm paradise, densely populated by snakes, relatives, spirits, monkeys, and gods.

I was a foreigner. I could not buy real estate or stocks, and I was not allowed to enter many temples. But I lived here. I created jobs and paid taxes. I made mistakes. I said the wrong things. I ate with the wrong hand and the wrong way.... But I apologized. I smiled. I learned. I moved on.

On the way back to Bangalore, I felt that I was finally accepted into the family. Perhaps not as a close relative, but as, say, the beloved second cousin of the aunt's father-in-law. To me — an introverted nomad — even this kind of communion was sweeter than Mysore sweets.

The Offices and Mansions

We were hiring fast. When we reached more than

two hundred, the centrifugal forces and the rising rent catapulted us out of the posh Lavelle Road, in the heart of the city, to Koramangala, closer to the outskirts. Until recently, this was a swampy area with paddies and occasional farmhouses. Today it's a charming neighbourhood with shady streets where residents can even walk, which is a real luxury for Bangalore.

For my personal accommodation, I was lucky to rent a magnificent house relatively inexpensively. It was proudly rising in the very centre of the Shiva Garden compound — a luxurious green oasis in the midst of Bangalore's hustle and bustle. The mansion was huge, spacious, and solemnly empty, like a cathedral. In the middle of the vast living room, infrequent guests were perplexed by an intricate fountain turned into a flowerbed and by a mysterious glass structure next to it. Stunned foreigners usually took it for a glass shower or an elevator. They were close, as minds (not bodies) were both elevated and purified there — it was a traditional "puja room," where lonely but cheerful little Lord Ganesha was comfortably working on his laptop.

Sometimes the vultures would drop clean, pale chicken skins of unknown origin from their celestial height right on my porch, either as an offering or a warning.

My home was like a ship in the Bay of Shiva, separated from the breakers of the Bangalore ocean by a wide and fetid drain. The bay was guarded by huge kites nesting in magnificent trees, and Alice, a frowning bully of a cat. This creature, while a male by all indications, would bring a litter of charming red kittens a couple times a year. They frolicked in the grass like mischievous oranges. Alas, the kittens never survived, no matter how hard my neighbours in Shiva Garden and I tried to help them. It's hard to be a little kitty in a land of stray dogs, rats, and snakes.

The imposing mansion was too large for me, like a jacket size five hundred (UK measurement). Our new office building turned out too small, as we continued to grow rapidly. Less than a month after our house-warming puja, when all the monitors were decorated with large orange dots (*tilaks*), we began spilling over around Koramangala like boiled-over milk, renting a floor here and a floor there, whatever we could get.

Elephant at a Corporate Party

Our "Annual days" — the MCR India corporate birthday celebrations and kick-offs — sealed the previous year and set the pace for the next. Every December, we invited our CEO and his team to Bangalore. Other colleagues came uninvited, combining their love of India with their love of currying top management: it was easier to catch Ron in Bangalore than in London.

Well, the more, the merrier.

Our presentations had to be crisp, as patience had never been our CEO's forte. When Ron got bored (usually on the very first slide of any PowerPoint deck), he would start rotating his hands in the air, which meant, "Roll on, spin the wheels, move on, I've already got it!"

Ron's signature rotating windmill gesture trained us not to talk about what was interesting to us but about what was important to the audience.

In other words, almost nothing.

On the last day of a kick-off week, we used to take the entire company, hundreds of people by that time, to a resort in the outskirts of Bangalore. Roles reversed there: executive team members presented to our crowd. Some presentations were corporate-boring to the extreme. I was looking at Ron, hoping he'd save us with his trademark rotating sword gesture, but he was busy writing emails on his mobile, reminding me of Ganesha with a laptop.

At the entrance to the resort, guests were greeted by a team of half-naked Theyyam-style drummers, who beat out a dry, rhythmic beat. Some were leading the main line — male, deep, rumbling, and rhythmic. Others were scattering a subtle, rapid, unsettling female beat that was going up and coming down, curling around the main rhythm like ivy. Or just like we in India were curling around the main MCR sites.

Every year we tried something new. Once, Ron was

taken for a ride in an Indian village bullock cart. Ron wasn't thrilled; he said the cart reminded him of his early childhood in Romania.

Assuming that Ron's Romanian childhood was deprived of elephants, we hired a lavishly decorated temple elephant next year. Alas, the poor animal was suffering from indigestion. Or, perhaps, it was enjoying good digestion. In any case, our guests preferred to keep a distance.

Meanwhile, our guys admired the elephant, the cart, and the CEO. We were a young company; energy, laughter, and a certain naivete were our competitive advantage.

At one of the management trainings, we were told about the three ideal qualities: a perfect employee should be hungry, humble, and smart. All our overseas colleagues were smart as hell and hungry for work like wolves, but humility was in short supply. In India, I found untapped deposits. We could build a good business on humility if it were properly mined and processed.

From the stage, I announced: "MCR India is a software factory and an ego-free development centre. An Indian proverb says, 'I am Rajah, you are Rajah — who will go fetch water?' We will bring the water to the MCR Maharajas!"

I made my presentation light, with funny photos of our people, who were so happy to see themselves on the big screen. After endless photo-sessions with the CEO awards' winners, we had a concert by our employees: folk dancing, songs, and skits, picking on our management, our bossy colleagues from overseas, and ourselves. The guy impersonating me on stage sounded and looked so much better than me that I was seriously concerned about my job security.

The drive to create something innovative, exciting, and beautiful transitioned from this festive stage to our workstations. The echoes of our songs reverberated in our office hallways for months. Annual day was a creativity booster shot.

Traditionally, the evening ended with a disco. I pretended that I had no clue why the endless chain of our programmers was stretching to the dusty parking lot.... Taught by past bitter experience, we did not serve booze, so our prudent guys refuelled themselves with the alcohol stocked in their cars and bikes.

Overseas guests were served drinks without restrictions, so everyone danced joyfully and recklessly, laughing as even children no longer laugh in the West.

"I'm glad we have more Indians than chiefs now," Ron said to me in a deep purring voice, glancing at the flock of his VPs. "If your guys write code as well as they dance, they are the future!"

In modest traditional India, there are no partner dances. Our VPs were prancing Punjabi dances with the clumsy diligence of neophytes. But they were not even close to our guys.

Of course, we delivered. When deliveries are botched, no singing or dancing helps. But when it's all about deliveries, there is nothing much to deliver.

The day after the corporate party, I received an email from the electrician-goddess. He inquired about a job — he would do anything.

I politely declined. We needed developers and testers, not gods. I had to throw myself into the corporate fire and dance on burning coals all by myself.

PART II. SOFTWARE VARANASI

Software Varanasi

"Don't get me wrong, Vladi," said Alex, an old friend of mine and our software guru from Jerusalem, sipping his favourite Scotch at my house. "I like working with your guys. They are ready to listen, easy to talk to, and hard working. But they are not passionate about software as an art form. Instead, they are passionate about fast promotions."

I kept refilling his glass melancholically. There was not much to argue about. Indeed, in the West, one can retire as a software developer — an individual contributor. In densely populated, hierarchical India, that would be considered a failure. Here, you are as good as the number of people reporting to you. They say the word "Manager" on a business card entitles a man to a bigger dowry from a bride's parents. A "Director" or "VP" designation is worth even more on the matrimonial market.

I liked a linear correlation between the number of subordinates and a number of buffalos a man can get as a dowry. Herd for herd, developers for buffalos — simple and straightforward. I enquired about my personal matrimonial worth. Alas, it was null. Foreigners were always expected to pay in India. Without hope of getting a herd or two, I had to stick to my job for a living.

"India is good for support and maintenance. I am not going to move new product development to you," Alex gave his verdict. "Cheers! Le Chaim!"

What a waste of good Scotch. True, although many computer geniuses hail from India, India had positioned itself as the world's capital of maintenance and support.

For a hard-core developer, writing a new system is the coolest challenge — the opposite of boring maintenance of an already deployed system. Those brilliant minds who create software don't like supporting it. It's tedious. Someone else can do it.

Enter India, with its tradition of maintenance and support. This tradition got a boost towards the end of the twentieth century. The world was expected to end at midnight, January 1, of the new millennium. Satan was not to blame, for a change. This time, lazy software developers had done the damage. In the most vital of systems, the years were encoded with only the last two digits (e.g., "97" instead of "1997"). Those digits were about to reset to "00" in the year 2000 (or Y2K for short), causing the stock exchanges and transport networks to collapse, and the gates of hell to open.

Software engineers had to go through hundreds of millions of lines of legacy code to fix the date encoding and prevent Doomsday. For picky Western programmers, it was tedious in the extreme. Indian engineers — inexpensive, unassuming, and patient enough for this monotonous work — came to the rescue.

Indeed, the very idea of patience is different in India.

My friend came here to study yoga with one of the local masters. The master instructed her to do one hundred and eight repetitions of "Surya Namaskara" ("salutation to the Sun" — a series of traditional postures and moves) every morning. After a couple of weeks, she was on the brink of a nervous breakdown.

"Please tell me what else I can do," she asked the master. "Doing the same thing every morning is sooo boring!"

"Don't worry — it is only boring for the first five years," the master replied.

The line-by-line decoding and deciphering of the spaghetti code was not an issue for the diligent and patient Indian developers. While saving the world, they learned a lot about legacy software systems and started taking over their maintenance. The Indian software industry was born not out of the beautiful lotus flower of a scientific breakthrough but the coarse hogweed of tedious bug fixing on a planetary scale.

Bug Y2K had convinced the captains of the software industry in the West that India was the right place for low-end work and maintenance. Indian industry had eagerly accepted this role, turning itself into a dumping ground for Western software. More precisely, into an IT Varanasi.

Varanasi is the holiest of the seven sacred cities in India. Old people come to this ancient place from all over India to die in peace. Passing away in this sacred place is the shortest way out of Samsara. When the time comes, a family gathers money for their old man's or woman's last journey. Arriving in Varanasi, the old people have no more than two weeks to conclude their earthly existence at a special hotel; otherwise, they risk running out of money. Returning home undead is both a financial burden and a terrible shame: an old person is supposed to kick the bucket when their time has come.

The souls of those who pass away at Varanasi are successfully reincarnated or liberated. The corpses are burned, and the charred bits and ashes are thrown into the Ganges river.

India is to software what Varanasi is to old people: a good place to die. Corporations send ageing and ailing systems to India to spend a couple of years in austerity, without a budget for new development, getting ready to bite the dust. In the meantime, Western developers write new and much more advanced software to replace the legacy one.

This is what we call "progress".

Introducing Evo

Once, on a weekend trip to the ancient town of Hampi, I was crossing the river in a coracle, a round leather-covered boat that looked like a round sled from my childhood. And then, out of the blue of the Indian skies, a mighty eagle pooped on my worry-laden head. Thankfully, my head was covered by a colonial Panama hat. The accuracy of the hit indicated that it was deliberate, so I took it as a blessing.

The next day, my boss, Yossi — senior VP Development — called to inform me that the management had decided to fully transfer Evo to India for support.

Evo is a software stack for set-top boxes (STBs). The STB is a small computer attached to a TV. Subscribers receive it from satellite or cable broadcasters when they subscribe to their services. An STB receives video and audio signals from a satellite dish or a cable connection, does some magic with it, and sends the decoded picture and voice to the TV. Subscribers expect a dazzling experience on their gorgeous TV screens. The electronic program guide (EPG) and interactive apps should look slicker and perform smoother than Apple product. No one cares that it is not the modern and sleek TV that is doing the heavy lifting but the little clumsy box next to it.

The STB is the least appreciated of all consumer electronic devices at home. It is far less sexy than a fridge or a microwave. No one has ever tried to impress a girlfriend or a neighbour with a new STB, so no one wants to pay for it, and no one loves it. Yet, without it, there is no broadcast video. Many people these days "cut the cord," but there are still hundreds of millions who rely on this device. Despite all the hype about cord-cutting, their number is growing.

STB is a piece of hardware, so it needs software to power it. This was where Evo came into play. Evo was a big ugly chunk of software of more than five million lines of code powering unsexy legacy devices that are expected to provide the best user experience possible.

MCR didn't produce hardware. STBs were manufactured by third-party vendors, mostly Korean, Polish, and Chinese. Dependencies on hardware and drivers didn't make our lives easier.

For MCR India, Evo (short for Evolution) was an

adopted child. It was first developed in the UK, toward the end of the previous century, as an experiment of sorts. The key business of MCR was securing access to video transmission, so the software stack for STBs was a new domain.

After gaining traction with the first Evo customers, MCR management got serious about this business. But Evo was not intended for scaling up. It had already been contaminated with poor maintenance, and become a victim of early ageing.

MCR business was booming, so money was not an issue. Ron could afford to invest big in a shiny new product to replace Evo. The new product was named Neo, predictably enough. Like its namesake, the hero of The Matrix, Neo would evade the customers' bullets and use the elegant ballet steps of martial arts to destroy competitors. The best developers in the UK, Israel, and France had already started working on Neo.

To free up resources in the UK for the new development, management decided to transfer maintenance of the legacy Evo to India. When Neo was ready, Evo should die in peace in our software Varanasi of Bangalore.

There was also a political side to the transfer: our site in India had already proven its mettle in maintenance, working closely with project managers in the UK. British project managers found it more comfortable to work with malleable and smiley Indian developers than with their compatriots, whom they found too inflexible, cocky, and focused on writing beautiful software rather than serving their customers.

That is how, after a minor earthquake in our corporate skies, Evo landed on us. We didn't ask for it — UK project managers did our job for us. As the Jewish saying goes, "The work of the righteous is done by others."

I had been a site leader and general manager of MCR India, looking after our "colonial" French, UK, and Israeli lines, as well as HR, IT, admin, finance, and my favourite travel department. Now I had become the owner of a newly established Evo division.

Agile and Yoga Masters

There was a somewhat sad note to my joy: I was a bit embarrassed about Evo. Apart from a few common software components, most of its code was written for each client individually. Serious developers like me disdain client-specific code. We aim higher, to create a generic solution suitable for all customers, for all occasions, and for all eternity.

And in a year or two, we develop a new, even more eternal and generic system.

But, alas, with our four customers, the cost of a generic solution could exceed the savings from generality and flexibility. Besides, Neo was developed from scratch as one system for all customers. There was no point in rewriting Evo for its short remaining life-span. As soon as Neo took off, Evo would hand over its customers and give its soul to the software gods.

I was fascinated by the free spirit of Agile and the minimalist aesthetic of the "lean" approach: do only what is required, only when it is required. Do not strive for perfection and do not try to second-guess the future — no matter how forward-thinking you are, the Universe will always find ways to surprise you. Speed and flexibility are more important than perfection!

In these ideologically confused times, some in the West are wondering, how could seventeen middle-aged white American men, by themselves, come up with anything of value, if their team was not diverse?

But these dudes didn't invent anything. They simply applied eternal ideas to software — as a line of thought, Agile is much older than the Manifesto.

Our CEO, Ron, liked to quote Napoleon Bonaparte, "Let's engage in the battle; then we'll figure out how to win it!" This sounds pretty Agile, doesn't it?

Or maybe Jesus, not Napoleon, was the first Agilist? Jesus said, "Do not worry about tomorrow, for tomorrow will worry about itself." Cross that bridge when you come to it. Solve today's problem today, slice it thin. Don't try to predict the future. Instead, do something small and tangible, and correct course every day — this is the essence of Agile.

Lord Ganesha — like every Scrum Master — is called "a remover of obstacles."

The spirit of Agile was pounding in my heart. The pragmatic, lean way suited us in India surprisingly well. I explained it to my boss, Yossi, with the following story, which I heard somewhere:

> An Indian spiritual master was meditating on the bank of a river. Another guru, wanting to impress him, crossed the river, walking on the water as if it were land. Once he crossed the river that way, he asked the first holy man:
>
> "Did you see what I just did?"
>
> "Sure! You walked on the water. Where did you learn this skill?"
>
> "Oh, I spent twelve years in the Himalayas doing yoga. I fasted six days a week, standing on one foot all day," the second sage replied proudly.
>
> "But why bother so much? Our ferryman can take you across the river for just two paise!" wondered the first one.

As a Western engineer, I wanted to create beautiful products and walk on water. As an Indian manager, I wanted to be a boatman: move every client, fast, in the spirit of Agile — and earn a couple of coins on the way.

So we decided to develop solutions for each client separately, copy-pasting code from one project to another if needed. This approach is nauseous for any hard-core developer. But, in our case, it was cheaper than heavy and expensive "productization."

I was flipping through the Tao Te Ching. "Soft and flexible" bends without breaking — and adapts to market changes and corporate disasters. As Darwin said, "It is not the strongest of the species that survives, nor the most intelligent; it is the one most adaptable to change."

Corporate Alchemy

It was our best time ever. We were doing what we liked, and we were good at it.

In our Western centres, everyone wanted to lead others, as if leadership was the shortest path to salvation. In a world full of "leaders," Indian engineers were invaluable. Instead of engaging in intellectual show-offs and ego fights, they were following our customers, Indian cultural patterns, and the Agile spirit. They were also following Evo project managers from the UK, to their utmost delight. Project managers could sprint forward with their teams, neither depending on each other nor on one "generic" product.

I had built the Evo management team on the age-old proven principles — those of alchemy. Since everything is made up of four elements, fire, water, earth, and air, our team's composition was the same.

My first two elements had joined us the same auspicious day.

Manoj's ability to flow around obstacles and avoid conflicts reminded me of the element of water. No matter what, he was as calm as water in a glass. Thin as a teenager, not wearing a typical Indian moustache, with aristocratic features and long, slender fingers, Manoj looked like a poet or a philosopher. He was partly both: he loved Buddhism and Osho's philosophy, and he also composed courtly Urdu poems in the spirit of Omar Khayyam. After a fair amount of his favourite single malt Scotch, Manoj never refused to read his poems to his awestruck listeners.

Born and brought up in Enterprise Java, Manoj naturally gravitated towards management. I had asked him to work with Evo project managers from overseas, but soon Manoj had started nurturing his own Evo project management office, in addition to Evo integration and testing.

Padma was the element of fire in my corporate alchemy. When in a good mood, she vibrated, sparkled and radiated energy sufficient to light up a mid-sized city. When she was not in the mood, that same energy could burn that city to ashes. The electrified air around her always smelled of ozone.

Before moving into management (which she often regretted), Padma was a workaholic developer and an architect. In the days of our corporate childhood, I used to stay up late in my fish tank office. One night, going to the pantry for a cup of tea, I saw Padma sitting at her desktop.

"Padma, isn't it time for you to go home? It's already late."

"Vladi, I have to make a release today! Alex is waiting!"

"Trust me, I know Alex, and I know the context: he can easily wait till tomorrow! Please go home!"

Padma didn't reply — she was on the brink of sobbing.

Forty minutes later, I went out for another cup of tea. To my surprise, Padma was still frantically tapping at the keyboard, this time together with her young husband, a developer from another company. Padma killed two birds with one stone: she released the code on time, just before midnight — and made sure her husband was not bored or cross with her. Pair programming works best!

At Evo, Padma was responsible for component development, including the user interface. Our water and fire got along quite well — working together with Manoj was never an issue for Padma.

Shalini, who had joined later, was our element of earth. Reliable, balanced, and mature, always ready to support and comfort, she was our organizational mother and moral compass.

Once during our "one-on-one," Shalini spotted a new t-shirt on my desk, still wrapped in crisp cellophane. These t-shirts had recently been distributed to a team, marking successful delivery of their project.

"Vladi, I'm sorry, but why did you take this t-shirt?"

"What do you mean 'why'? To wear it, of course. It was given to everyone."

"But you didn't work on the project, so why did you take it?"

I was speechless. I thought Indian engineers respected hierarchy.

"Hmm.... Well, you know, I'm the boss, after all; I helped... with, umm... vision and strategy... and with free lunches! Don't you think I deserve this shirt for all my efforts?"

"As you wish, Vladi. I wouldn't take it if I were you."

I thanked Shalini for her advice. As for the t-shirt, it had become my favourite.

If Manoj was the element of water, Padma was fire, and Shalini was earth, I had the only choice left, and it suited me well. I was the element of air: always in flight, in motion, constantly creating turbulence — and the first one to suffer from it.

Victims of Our Own Success

Our ageing Evo was sent to the Varanasi of Bangalore, but it was not granted the luxury of dying: Neo, our young and beautiful angel of death, was chronically late. We did not rush it — we kept growing. Our lean, agile approach hit the bull's eye, so new customers popped up every month. We used to set up new teams for them, and they worked so well that our customers smiled at us.

It's amazing how quickly our advantages turn into problems. We kept growing — but we were not ready for this cheerful and reckless growth. Slowly but surely, we became the victims of our own success.

We had to copy-paste every feature and fix every bug as many times as we had customers. When the number and complexity of features, as well as the number of clients, increased, this approach blew up in our faces. What worked well with four clients didn't work well with twelve. The practices of a team of forty were not good for a team of two hundred.

The market was also changing. Customers expected standard features to be delivered to them right away. They didn't get why we had to re-develop something that already worked for others.

The world was changing, but we were stuck. Talking about "embracing the change," we carried on in the same direction, pouring in more and more "resources" to fix issues. After all, our engineers cost a penny compared to Western ones. And my managers traditionally measured their success by the number of subordinates.

It was a Catch-22. The more we hired, the more chaotic and inefficient the system became — forcing us to hire even more people. Our best engineers spent time teaching, guiding, managing others, and fixing their code. They were muddling through endless discussions and meetings instead of writing software. Everyone was so busy that they had no time for work. Instead of practicing non-doing, I was engaged in endless firefighting. Evo was gradually getting slower, buggier, and messier.

Following our customers and stakeholders, we had created a flow — and its gushing current was carrying our boat straight onto the reefs. I wanted to be the boatman from the parable, but "being in the flow" requires more than "going with the flow." We had to learn to use the winds and currents to move against them.

Simply said, we had to do what I had previously refused to do: we had to "productize" Evo, carving out a single product out of many projects.

Relocation Gone Wrong

At that time, there was not enough product development expertise in Bangalore: only five to ten percent of the companies led their own products. The rest "provided services." To productize Evo, I had to strengthen the team and infuse it with fresh architectural blue blood.

That's why I convinced Martin, a brilliant architect with proven product experience, to relocate to Bangalore for a year. Lanky and energetic, Martin was charged up and looking for adventures, so convincing him didn't take long. Like many architects, Martin had unshakably strong opinions about technology and architecture, as well as life, the Universe, and everything else. Obviously, Martin understood Indian culture much better than the Indian people themselves.

Some foreigners hate India. They vaccinate themselves against all diseases known and unknown, even if the side effects are worse than the diseases. Foreign weaklings faint at mere trifles, such as bloody religious self-mutilation. Or just at watching the everyday life of the Mumbai slums from an air-conditioned car, as happened with one of our project managers from the UK.

Others, like Martin, fall in love with India. Martin

started wearing kurtas instead of shirts, and dhoti (local loincloth) instead of pants — thankfully, not in the office. He had mastered the art of the Indian head bobble. He greeted people with his two palms folded into "Namaste," a gesture I had only seen before in five-star hotels and temples. At a speed slightly faster than light, he travelled all across India from Ladakh to Kanyakumari.

Alas, Martin's love for India remained unrequited. "He thinks that India is shallow, that it can be easily imitated. But he is a phony," Padma, whom he apparently liked, told me.

I was hoping that Martin would not just lead the productization of Evo — he would also show my team what technical excellence, proactivity, and assertiveness mean.

And show them he did. Martin instructed and put pressure, explaining how components should be rewritten, how teams should be restructured, and how the Indo-Pakistani conflict should be resolved. The engineers did not argue with him; they smiled amiably and wobbled their heads. This wonderful head wobble sets the rhythm of the conversation, its "carrier frequency." It confirms that the communication line has been established: "Carry on, I like you, mate."

In no way does it mean an agreement with the message.

Our pleasantly smiling developers flowed around

Martin like the water of a river around a huge boulder in its middle. Our managers parted in front of Martin, like the ocean waves before the heavy hull of the Titanic.

Martin was not invited to meetings anymore. Others could not attend those meetings he set up — they were terribly sorry, but matters of the utmost importance prevented them. The gushing stream of corporate emails in Martin's mailbox dried to a trickle. Deprived of organizational oxygen — information — Martin couldn't stay in India any longer.

The Tao Te Ching was spot on, as always. It was a sad victory of "soft" over "hard" — organizational antibodies won without a fight. The obstacle had been removed, and the opportunity of improving Evo's architecture was lost.

Murali, my chief architect, walked around sighing despondently — whoever was to blame, it wasn't him.

All of it was my mistake. I should have plugged Martin into our system, giving him a team to manage. But Martin did not want to report to Murali, and I did not want to take Murali's people and give them over to Martin. Instead, I had defined a vague role for Martin reporting directly to me — and it backfired.

Martin's departure was bitter for me but sweeter than honey for our finance department. As adventurous as self-confident, Martin insisted on driving the company-provided car himself. We ended up paying more in damages for his numerous accidents than for a whole year of a driver's service.

Martin's departure made our financial director so happy that he splurged for a parting gift out of his own pocket: a Ganesha figurine holding a laptop.

To productize Evo, we had to rely on local talents — ourselves.

Boys and girls

Relocations and frequent trips are part of life in an international company.

We rented a serviced apartment for young engineers we sent to the UK so that they could cook some proper Indian food and feel better together — and reduce hotel costs for us, too.

Spoiled by their Desi moms and tipsy with foreign freedom, our guys did not take proper care of their house, damaging furniture and bathroom fixtures. The enraged landlord threatened to sue the company. Our UK office agreed to settle. We had to pay 3,600 pounds in damages.

Had girls lived in this apartment, everything would have been fine. Peter Pan was right, saying, "...One girl is more use than twenty boys." Girls in an Indian male-dominated environment are often better prepared for the realities of life. Why?

Money is a major factor, as usual. The birth of a daughter is a financial misfortune for poor families. She will eventually leave home to care for her husband's family, but a hefty dowry has to be paid to marry her off! A son brings wealth to the family; a daughter takes wealth away.

Poor families sometimes turn to abortions to avoid the financial burden of growing a daughter. More boys are born in the country than girls. The government bans disclosing the sex of an unborn child, but the black market for ultrasound scans is thriving.

India is dominated by men — or so men think. Parents are proud of their sons, who are going to inherit the wealth and continue the line. No wonder boys often grow up pampered. Stories of a fight between two boys — pupils at a good Bangalore school — were on the front pages of local newspapers for almost a week, so extraordinary it was: good boys seldom fight in India. While the sons are often spoiled, the daughters work hard from their cradle caring for others in the family.

My Russian friend visited her in-laws in their village, along with her husband, an Indian investment banker. To her utter surprise, she found out that women were not allowed to sit down to eat with men — women and girls served during meals and then ate the leftovers. When my friend proudly mentioned that she had just signed up for the gym, her Indian mother-in-law was upset, "Why would you do that, eh? A woman must bear children and take care of her husband, not fool around in the gym!"

Gradually, fitness for women was getting socially acceptable. We had kickboxing classes in the gym near my house, in addition to yoga and aerobics. I was the only male in the group. Several guys had started but dropped out — classes were too tough. But the women persevered. They sweated, puffed, punched, and kicked me as hard as they could. What doesn't kill women makes them stronger — literally.

The same patterns were at play at our office. Padma — my element of fire — was a disruptor and a fighter. Shalini was a harmonizer, but she could stand her ground — she was an element of earth. Manoj, my guru and designated heir to the throne, yielded and flowed around like water, avoiding conflicts.

Engine: Choosing Between Right and Right

To productize Evo, we had to reduce the duplication of effort by carving out more shared components from customer code branches. Padma and her small team started rewriting code in line with the new architecture blessed by Murali — our chief architect.

We called those shared components *engine*.

The *engine*'s goal was to improve our time-to-market. Ironically, *engine* development itself was chronically late — we had underestimated the scope of the work, as we had never done anything like that before.

Manoj was not an ardent proponent of productization, to put it gently. He thought we were rowing against the current for nothing — Neo would soon be ready.

He volunteered to fix the project mess without changing the architecture but only if Padma's commando engineers were transferred from the *engine* to his customer projects. I trusted Manoj; he always walked the talk.

"How many times can we apologize for delays? It's high time for us to put ambitions aside and acknowledge that product development is not our cup of tea. Agile likes failing small; adaptability is about course correction, not stubbornness," I told Padma during our regular weekly one-on-one.

I had to choose my words carefully if I didn't want to get burnt. Padma — an element of fire — was passionate about her job, as if the fate of the Universe depended on it. They say Indian engineers are soft and unable to say "no." Padma was more Israeli than Israelis, ready to pick any fight, any time.

Her black eyes filled with gleaming lava.

"No, Vladi, we can't give up! This is wrong! What if

Neo is late by another three years? I want us to have a product! I'll do everything, I promise you!"

Static electricity crackled in the room. A hole smoked in my virtual bulletproof vest.

Manoj was right. Padma was right, too.

I love the ancient joke about a rabbi who was asked to settle a dispute between two neighbours. The rabbi listened to the first neighbour and said, "Chaim, you're right!" Then, after hearing out the second neighbour, he concluded, "Moshe, you're right." The rabbi's outraged wife shouted at her husband, "Hey, they can't both be right at the same time!" The rabbi stared thoughtfully at his wife and sighed heavily, "You know, Sarah, you're right, too!"

Rabbis' and managers' jobs are so fascinating because everyone is right, but it is up to them to make choices. Was Manoj overcautious and conservative? Or "down-to-earth" and pragmatic? Was Padma unduly aggressive and ego-driven? Or committed and passionate?

We would get to know only post-factum. Or rather, post-mortem.

"What about non-doing?" Manoj asked me a few months later. "You don't like acting by brute force, do you? Why did you let Padma do it?"

"Well, Padma is a force of nature, so she creates her own flow. Non-doing is about directing flows, not hampering them. That's my job."

Corporate reality is much better at clarifying philosophical concepts than is scholarly analysis. I've always been fascinated by the idea that the future determines the past. Padma's "stubbornness" miraculously turned into "persistence" after months of hard work, when the *engine* was eventually deployed. Had Padma not delivered, she would have retroactively become "stubborn and inflexible."

Platform: Monkeys and Buffaloes

In an ideal world, Evo would be one product for all customers, like a refrigerator. In the real world, we had about twenty clients — TV broadcasters all around the globe. Their target audiences were different; the tastes of their chief marketing officers (and their spouses) varied too.

A single product was ruled out. Delivering a separate version for every customer would be too slow and expensive, so it was also ruled out.

During his brief solo act in India, Martin was pushing for the "platform + custom" model: a large team develops a generic platform. Small customization teams adapt it to different customers.

One of the MCR products in our UK line was developed using this very model. It was non-stop fighting. Client teams waited for months for the platform to wake up and do what their customer wanted. The platform, striving to be generic, was irritated by silly customers' requests for specific features.

What should we do? "Platform + custom" is a reasonable model from the architectural perspective. But what should our teams' structure be?

At that time, we were organized into a classical matrix: engineers were divided into development, integration, and testing departments. Within development, teams were organized by software components. Out of all those departments, Manoj's project managers carved out virtual teams for specific customers.

Manoj suggested that we let the client teams develop the functionality, each for its own customer, but in such a way that other client teams could easily use the same code later. In the classic model, the mighty buffalo — the platform team — pulls the product forward, and nimble, small client teams follow like monkeys. We turned this model around. The generic Evo platform was pulled by our buffaloes — client teams. The platform team was a small monkey directing client teams and cleaning up after them.

We in India worked better for customers than for a "generic" product. The Evo platform cart started rolling, led by our big clients. The product roadmap was a sum total of all customer features.

Our development was carried out directly on the

"trunk" of the code. We did not allow code to branch out, as merging it back into the trunk was a pain in the neck. The platform team kept constantly testing the code trunk so that we could use it for a new customer at any time, selecting features à la carte.

We couldn't believe ourselves when we delivered to a new customer in Greece in two and a half months — it used to take us six months or more!

One thing dimmed our joy: that tiny customer quietly went bankrupt after six months.

Stalin and Black Magic

Meanwhile, office life went on.

Our Stalin made a career and had deservedly become the chief "office boy." Still, he aspired to more, as in addition to administrative skills, Stalin also possessed some occult powers. At least that was what he told everyone, from sceptical Rajesh the driver to gullible Mary.

Mary Kulkarni, a mother of three kids with somewhat unexpected names — Michael Bush Kulkarni, Michael Clinton Kulkarni, and Mel Gibson Kulkarni — joined Stalin's team as a janitor. She had to work hard to support her family after the sudden disappearance of her husband, Mr. Kulkarni. It does happen in India that husbands disappear, re-emerging in other parts of the country under new names, often with new wives.

Since it was almost impossible to find a runaway husband in this vast subcontinent by conventional means, Mary consented to Stalin's offer of black magic.

Astrology and magic are tightly woven into the fabric of daily Indian life. From time to time, decapitated roosters are found on the streets of Bangalore, an ominous sign. It means someone is trying to cast a spell on his or her neighbour.

Ritual sacrifices are a part of the game. Once a father of three invited his wife, their daughters, and a neighbour with her child to go for a walk by one of Bangalore's lakes. Only the neighbour managed to escape. All of the others were drowned by the man, who had followed the advice of a local sorcerer: to find a treasure, you need to kill six women.

Stalin's magic was less radical. At Mary's place, he asked her to fetch him the photos and personal belongings of her husband. As a ritual sacrifice, he was ready to accept Mary's physical affection.

Mary was lucky to escape. She even found the courage to complain to our HR department — a very rare case in India in those days. There was no point in going to the police. It would do more harm than good. The only thing we could do was to fire Stalin immediately.

I had to make my own tea. But I was happy for Mary. Besides, I got an idea for a title for my future book, "I fired Stalin."

In the good old days, writers were paid. The world has changed. Writing, like pornography, has become a ubiquitous commodity. Too many people are keen to expose themselves in an intimate act with words, even for free. "More than the calf wants to suck, the cow wants to give milk," says the Talmud. Now people are paid for reading, not writing. I wish I could leave the pages of my book clean to make it easier for my readers.

Rules and Stamps

We were about halfway through the platform's productization when our CEO, Ron, called me up again. There was yet another escalation from an Israeli customer. The quality of the latest Evo release was below the level of the Dead sea (which is below the sea level).

Ron interrupted my confused explanations.

"Vladi, I can accept it when my people make mistakes. But not the same mistake twice. I hope you see what I mean."

Sure, I did. This was the fifth time Ron had called. To make new mistakes, something had to be urgently changed in the Evo land.

One school of thought says that to get reproducible and predictable results, we need a "process" — a detailed cookbook, spelling out who does what, when, how, and why. If instructions are followed by the book, the project will be delivered on time, on budget, and with quality. Indian companies were proud of their ability to "work by the rules," proving it with maturity certificates like CMMI or ISO 9001.

To me, these certificates did indicate the quality — just not the quality of the software. They certified formal compliance of piles of documents, churned out by quality assurance departments, with standards set in a parallel universe. As a proponent of Agile's passionate revolt against BSSPs (Big Stupid Systems and Processes), I hated the bureaucratic nonsense of rules, many of which (heavy sigh) had tainted my Indian experience.

Visitors to apartment complexes and offices are required to register at the entrance in thick handwritten folios. The loooooong serial number of the laptop has to be written in a special column. However, no one checks it upon exit.

"Then why should I register my laptop?" I used to ask grumpily.

"These are the rules, sir," was the usual reply.

The word "rules" was pronounced with so much reverence as if all its letters were capital.

At many Indian airports, ragged and grim-faced moustachioed officers stamp boarding passes and baggage tags with blueish stamps. A couple of airport attendants check these stamps two meters away. Three other officers thoroughly examine the same stamps before a passenger is allowed to board the flight. When security measures are increased, they put as many as two stamps instead of one. These blurry bluish runes of bureaucracy inspire a primordial horror in me. I can only hope, terrorists are equally scared.

The huge ISO certification sign on the roof of the old Mumbai airport was visible even from outer space — and it was the worst airport I'd ever been to! These days, Indian airports are among the best in the world, with no quality certificates on display.

The bundles of documents required for my annual registration with the Foreigners Registration Office could barely fit into our minivan. I had to spend the whole day there to get a duly stamped certificate.

The bureaucracy scared me off, but my team kept shyly mentioning the "process." If it was working for others, why don't we try it out?

"Do you want our people to be real software engineers? Or 'office plankton' who turn off their brains and follow instructions to the letter?" I relentlessly attacked my faint of heart teammates in my crusade against bureaucracy. Under the spell of instructions, developers would work mindlessly, like sleepwalkers. Or like clerks in the Foreigners Registration Office!

Instead of unanimous support, I heard vague murmurs in response. I felt betrayed, as my Agile team was ready to follow the rules.

"Individuals and interactions over processes and tools," I chanted the first of the Manifesto's four values. That's exactly why we let our foreign project managers — smart and proactive engineers — lead our teams, not relying on bureaucratic "process."

And then I got that ugly escalation from our Israeli customer.

Shamanism and the Spirit of Agile

Our release was delayed, and the client was getting increasingly anxious. The project manager from the UK asked the Indian team to cut down on testing. His wish was the team's command. Software was released to the customer, but their quality engineer found three critical bugs within the first fifteen minutes of testing. The project manager apologized to the enraged CTO. "Sorry, our Indian team made the wrong decision about the scope of testing. It won't happen again."

That's when Ron called me up.

Strictly speaking, the project manager was right. My team did not formally roll up to him. Besides, he only "suggested" cutting corners; he did not instruct them to. So it was my team's wrong decision, not his. Unfortunately, our young tester from India was not an expert in semantic differences. No way he could say "no" to a senior Brit.

This wasn't the first time our "smart and proactive engineers" did something really stupid.

"The process could give us clarity and define responsibilities. It could help us do the right thing," Shalini suggested.

From the Agile perspective, it would be a step back. There are no "processes" or "rules" in Agile — it is a spirit and way of thinking. A mindset defining everything we do!

"What do you think about Scrum framework, Vladi?" asked Padma.

"I don't like it. Scrum Masters don't write code and don't manage teams. It's not that clear what exactly they do. Product Owners don't really own anything. And if you just rename meetings into 'stand-ups' and tasks into 'user stories,' it will change nothing."

"What Scrum?" Manoj supported me. "We depend on the Israeli components of conditional access. We depend on Korean drivers, hardware from China… Too many dependencies. For us, Scrum won't work, period."

But something had to be done. So I made an executive decision to define the process within the current paradigm in accordance with the spirit of Agile. But without the shamanism of Scrum. Worst case, the process would work. Best case, things would go wrong, and I could tell the team, "Aha! I told you so!" And laugh demonically.

Usually, the QA (quality assurance) department is responsible for implementing the process. Our QA department was led by Shalini.

"If Shalini's people define the process, developers and integrators will never accept it," Manoj warned. "They'd be cynical about 'yet another QA initiative.'"

Manoj had a point. When one team takes responsibility for a task, others feel it is neither their job, nor their problem. They delegate the headache to the "responsible" team. If QA started enforcing "their" process, others would resist, in accordance with Newton's Third Law.

"Yes, Manoj. The process will be successful only if all teams define it — together," Shalini unexpectedly agreed.

But "together"? What "together"? Our siloed teams were deep in trenches, waging positional wars. Violent border skirmishes erupted. And then engineers crawled back to their grim organizational bunkers. Open battles were few.

"What about a good fight?" suggested Padma, dreamily extending her virtual claws. "Let teams vent their steam. We'll see what happens next."

This was how we got into "The Big Fight."

The Big Fight and Non-Doing

In about a week, we invited representatives from all teams — about forty engineers — to a small hotel in Koramangala, close to my Shiva Garden mansion.

Indian teams always take pride in their good work. To avoid big-time self-praising, we asked teams to answer just two questions during their fifteen minutes of fame:

> "What issues do other teams have with you?"

> "What issues do you have with other teams?"

"What's in a name?" Actually, quite a lot. We called the meeting "The Big Fight," and a Big Fight we got. A non-Indian, dealing with soft and smiley Indian engineers, can hardly imagine how harsh with each other they can be.

Everyone was right — from their own perspective:

Integrators and testers were blaming architects for not involving them earlier in the project lifecycle. Testers were accusing developers of poor quality and defensive attitudes. Developers were screaming back at testers for lack of understanding of their code. Integrators were mad that component teams didn't support them, just throwing their components over the fence. Architects were angry at everyone, especially the managers. I am not sure about other companies, but our architects were spectacularly grumpy.

When the "The Big Fight" was about to turn into a small brawl, Shalini gently asked me to step out of the room: she was embarrassed of our people in front of me — a foreigner.

I waited outside impatiently, checking my email and watching the lean palm squirrels scurrying around the hotel courtyard with a terribly busy look on their faces. To resist the temptation of going back to the meeting room and telling people how they should work, I went home, texting Shalini to call me up when the storm was over.

I felt out of place in the solemn silence of my airy home in the middle of the busy day. In search of calm, I flipped through the Tao Te Ching.

He who strides too hard cannot go far.

Therefore, the sage acts by not-doing.

Indeed. I should stop fussing like the silly busy squirrels. Take more time to listen. Empty my cup and create a void. Find the balance. Stay in the flow. Give space to others and trust them...

"I do trust them. But for God's sake, how can they make decisions about the future of my program without me?" My ego was indignant, echoing the courtyard's shrill bird calls.

I was passing the time strolling from one room to another. In the third-floor bathroom, I found the tiny corpse of a squirrel with its paws tragically raised to the heavens, floating in a toilet. The poor thing apparently had taken its own life by drowning itself in this unexpected vessel of eternal rest. How the squirrel found its way there was a mystery.

I kept checking my mobile every five minutes, waiting for a message from Shalini.

Organizational Self-Awareness

Shalini called towards evening. I rushed back to the hotel meeting room. There were no dead bodies, to my relief. Not even bloodstains. People were silent, not comfortable to look at each other. Instead, they were all staring at a messy, perplexing diagram on the huge dusty whiteboard, as respectfully and solemnly as at a war hero's memorial.

What the heck?

Our issues were systemic, but before "The Big Fight," our engineers had not understood the "system." Each one only looked at their part of the notorious corporate mammoth. For testers, everything looked like the number of defects and the test coverage. For project managers, it was dates and "resources." We had no common language, no common frame of reference. Each team was sure that they were doing just fine, but others had to change.

I was told that, after the initial screaming and shouting had subdued, Shalini started drawing this messy picture of what it took to deliver a feature across all stages, from requirements to release.

An ancient Greek maxim of "Know thyself" (which is also one of the key motives of the Indian Upanishads) equally applies to people and organizations. The ugly diagram on the whiteboard was a self-portrait of our "system": our organizational mirror.

I recalled how the young Agni Theyyam performer, looking at himself in the mirror, recognized a goddess. By looking into this ugly diagram, the engineers recognized themselves — not as representatives of different teams, but partners in the same value stream. They recognized that problems were common — everyone had to change.

We had three Big Fights, each starting with screaming and shouting and ending with a more detailed diagram of our sufferings.

Then it was time to design our Nirvana-state operating model, or simply the "process." The way we would work in an ideal world. Engineers had formed cross-functional teams. These teams defined roles and responsibilities at each step, as well as the criteria for moving from one step to the next. They also defined our governance model: who was authorized to make what decisions, including exceptions.

Teams didn't use any sophisticated models or buzz-words. They moved ahead intuitively and naively, but everyone was engaged. Our Nirvana process emerged as the shared common sense of all teams, captured and written down by Shalini. She facilitated more than she led, and moderated more than she suggested. Often, Shalini made people believe that her ideas were their own; she was just writing them down.

Working yet not taking credit,

Leading yet not dominating.

The only thing left for me was to review the outcomes, make a few remarks (to make the point that even a boss can bring value, heh-heh), and thank the teams.

It took about two months to define the process.

Just one minor thing was missing. We had to persuade project managers in the UK, Israel, and Korea to work by our process. They considered themselves "leaders," and we wanted them to follow the rules — our rules.

I was stockpiling corporate ammunition for a long and bloody war.

Process Exoskeleton

But the war never started. Project managers felt the

same pain as we did. Giving up on their "freedom" in exchange for stable deliveries was a fair deal for them. Especially when they realized that Ron and Yossi were on our side (which I had taken care of in advance).

About seventy people from abroad and five hundred engineers from Bangalore got process training from Shalini. There was nothing much to teach Indian engineers — they had created this process themselves. Our people were very proud that this was "their" process, not the QA department's. And certainly not mine.

The process gave superpowers to our people. Now a junior engineer from Bangalore could tell a senior from overseas, "I wish I could do those strange things you ask for, like releasing half-tested software! But I have a process to follow. I can't break it without special approval from the top!"

Only three people at MCR could approve exceptions: Shalini, Yossi, and I. Not even Ron, heh-heh.

The process had become a common frame of reference and a stiff exoskeleton for our software engineers. A stereotype of "working by the rules" won over "following orders from seniors."

"If they give you ruled paper, write across," my mother taught me as a child. I wanted my people to write as I did, across, while they wrote beautifully along the lines! But there is no "along" or "across" on a blank sheet. The paper must first be lined with rules. This is what our process did.

Antoine de Saint-Exupéry, The Little Prince's author, whom I read in my early youth, suddenly became relevant again.

In the desert, he tells in one of his books, you are free to go wherever you want. But there is no freedom of choice there, as there is nothing to choose from. The void is the same in all directions. In a palace, there are rules and restrictions: walls, guards, and dungeons. But that's exactly why you are free to choose your way.

Choices are created by rules. A "ruled paper" of frameworks and processes provides a coordinate system of sorts.

I was afraid that we would become too bureaucratic. Following instructions and working by the book is bureaucracy, indeed, but not when the team writes this book all by themselves.

The whimsy spirit of Agile had built a nest in defining the waterfall process.

Too bad, my boss, Yossi, could not grasp the unfathomable wisdom of Laozi's non-doing and refused to pay me more the less I worked.

Love vs Bureaucracy

You never get bored working with people. We had enough stories for a Bollywood movie. One of many was about an epic battle between the HR and administration department for the golden key to our in-office "dorm room." This room was intended for those who were not feeling well at work and urgently needed to lie down. The key was stored in the Admin department's safe.

I suggested we use this room also for outstation candidates coming for job interviews, who needed to stay in Bangalore overnight. I didn't realize it would quite literally open the doors for... umm... unconventional usage of this space.

Our engineers interpreted the need for staying overnight quite broadly. So one good Samaritan got a key to the dorm room, thanks to connections with the right people. And then promptly handed it over to two couples in dire need of privacy.

How was this possible in chaste and virtuous India?

I have been told that ancient Indian sexual norms were rewritten by virtuous Mughal conquerors in the Middle Ages. To make the erotic carvings of ancient Hindu temples look more decent, they ordered the stone attributes of gender to be chipped off. Later, India adapted and accepted this moral censorship as its own. Hindu people still worship the lingam and yoni, but eroticism is now taboo. Explicit scenes are cut out of Western movies, just like "indecent" body parts were chopped off statues centuries ago. And it's not just eroticism; nudity is also unacceptable. Even inside the changing rooms at swimming pools, there are special booths for complete and final disrobing. One of my developers, a scion of a respectable brahmin family, once admitted that no one had ever seen him naked, not even his wife. Not even he himself.

So in terms of morality, today's India resembles a prim and proper Victorian England. "Kama Sutra? Yes, I have heard about it. The book is obscene! It is foreign. Probably American..."

"For every action there is an equal and opposite reaction," so the more society suppresses sexuality, the more powerful it becomes, breaking out like steam from a closed cauldron. The modest and pious traditional India is highly sexually charged. Relationships flourish in modern Indian offices. Young people want to taste and feel life in a way their parents never could. All sorts of things have happened in our company.

Once a few Indian managers were invited to the global MCR conference in Amsterdam. Some of them opted to enjoy the local art form — live sex shows — instead of the mandatory corporate gala dinner. This situation could not be ignored, so I asked our HR director to investigate it. It turned out that our unorthodox HR director himself, advised by his new local friend, Masha from Russia, had led the exclusive group to that cultural event.

Even with all my experience and tolerance, a non-standard use of the office dorm room by two couples was too much to bear. The admin department lost the epic battle, and the key was handed over to HR, which was led by a new and much more conventional HR director by that time. HR had established formal entry rules and introduced a stiff process. Parties in the dorm room stopped.

Truly, nothing can stand in the way of love — except bureaucracy.

Tolstoy and Bugs

No matter how many volumes Leo Tolstoy wrote, only Anna Karenina's sad shoes on the platform and the phrase "Happy families are all alike; every un-happy family is unhappy in its own way" remain in the popular culture.

In the IT world, on the contrary, happiness in differ-ent organizations looks different, while the pictures of unhappiness are very similar. Customers usually complain about time-to-market, quality, and costs, as well as "transparency" and "response to change" — or rather, the lack of them.

When we started Evo productization, our key concern was quality. A colony of bugs was the critical element of our ecosystem, like a colony of friendly bacteria in the human gut. Hundreds of people were paid to find them and keep meticulous census of their population. Others sentenced them to death. A few engineers carried out the sentence, while others nursed the new generation. Had a kind but reckless fairy resolved all our bugs overnight, the system would have come to a grinding halt.

Yossi, my boss and our senior VP of development, started his quality quest from Evo. We grew the fastest across MCR, and our bug population grew even faster than us. Our strength was a pragmatic good-enough approach, not a passion for code quality.

At one of our TGIF parties, I had raised the quality issue in a fiery speech. Later, after a couple of beers for encouragement, a group of exceptionally brave engineers cornered me, "Vladi, look how many bugs Microsoft and Oracle have! Why on earth are you saying that our nine hundred-something are too many?"

Go explain this to our customers and to Yossi, my dears. Yossi was no kind tooth(less) fairy; he demanded changes — ASAP.

First, Yossi wanted data — real data. Shalini, who headed our quality assurance, had defined tons of metrics. They included the number of defects represented in cumulative flow diagrams, test automation coverage, number of code branches, cyclomatic code complexity, defect density per thousand lines of code, and technical debt. We also measured delivery statistics (mostly, delays) for hundreds of projects. We were pretty damn proud of ourselves as we presented our metrics to Yossi.

That's where the problems started.

"When we didn't have the data, Yossi demanded it. Now that we do have the data, he says, 'This is eyewash and lipstick on a pig,'" Shalini remarked melancholically.

Exactly. Yossi didn't want to be confused with facts, and he didn't trust our numbers. Our very attempts to explain them and justify ourselves were, in his eyes, proof that we were cheating.

We were hoping that the corporate storm would calm down soon, but Yossi didn't stop. To make things worse, he even invited Alex from Jerusalem to be his trusted representative in India — his "eye of Sauron."

The Elephant and the Rabbit

Alex was the best man for thrashing us. He was always slightly ahead of the cutting edge of the latest software innovations. So no wonder his opinions changed often.

"Alex, but last week you were so confident about the very opposite of what you are saying now!"

"So what?" Alex was genuinely perplexed. "I've just

seen what Martin Fowler (or Alistair Cockburn, or His Holiness the Dalai Lama) said at the conference yesterday. You can't stop the world!"

Amazingly knowledgeable in software engineering, Alex was not burdened with excessive sympathy for developers who did not appreciate the true beauty of their craft. The excitement of the journey, not the destination, was his passion. His favourite joke was about a male rabbit chasing a female elephant: "If I don't catch her, at least I'll warm up." Our soft and clumsy elephant couldn't get away from Alex's sabre-toothed rabbit.

India is super-positive and hyper-emotional. In the palette of human relations, halftones and nuances are almost missing: if it's hatred, it's a deadly one. If it's love, it is passionate and eternal — even if only for a couple of days. The death of a favourite politician or a movie star causes mass riots and suicides — people can't live in a world where their idol is no more.

In offices, too, emotions roar; smashingly positive feedback is expected, even necessary, to keep people motivated.

Getting positive feedback from an Eastern European is scarcer than hen's teeth.

"Why should I praise my team for doing the right thing?" wonders an Eastern European manager. "If I am not scolding them, they should be happy!"

An Eastern European engineer expects a boss to

be unhappy by default. Receiving positive feedback often feels fake and suspicious: "Why is my boss praising me for nothing? There must be some dark conspiracy going on!" An Eastern European engineer is worried.

An Indian engineer is convinced that if the boss does not thank and praise everyone, then he or she must be extremely unhappy. This kills motivation and leads to depressions, allegations of "mental harassment and torture," and resignations.

"We've reduced the total number of bugs from 963 to 730 during the last quarter," our Indian engineer proudly told Alex, expecting the appreciation that a 25 percent improvement in quality deserves!

Thank you, this is an amazing result! — I silently prompted Alex in my mind.

"Are you kidding?" Alex hadn't heard me, and he was absolutely stunned. "What 'improvement' are you talking about? If your clients have to live with 700 bugs, how can you even sleep at night when your code is so crappy?"

After a minute of awkward silence, we moved on to the next metric.

"We've succeeded in keeping the total number of severe warnings below 200, as promised!" Another engineer reported with a slightly strained anxious smile.

"Tell me, how many of them are in the new code?" shot Alex.

My guys looked at each other. To keep the total number below the threshold, they had fixed minor issues in the old code, not complicated new ones. But still, they'd delivered on their commitments, hadn't they?

"Will you ever stop fooling Yossi and me?" Alex exploded. "You write crappy code and just play with numbers!"

My people were on the brink of a nervous breakdown; Shalini had to soothe and comfort our engineers, who were literally sobbing after video calls with Alex.

Indian offices are family-like: our teams expected us, their mangers, to stand up for them. Western organizations are formal. Yossi expected Indian managers to help him berate their teams. I was torn apart in a corporate split between the teams and the boss — both sides demanded unconditional loyalty.

I tried to explain, but Yossi just blindly backed Alex. The whole program had the unmistakable aura of being sanctioned by Ron himself.

That was my worst time at MCR India. Night after night, I dreamed that I was an ant crawling out of a sand crater. The faster I climbed, the faster the sand crumbled beneath me.

In my dream, I knew that a predator — an ant-lion — was waiting for me at the very bottom of the crater. I would wake up gasping and sweating.

The sand in the corporate hourglass poured quickly. When Yossi said that he was heading to Bangalore, I realized that my future at the company was on the line. Maybe my time was up.

Rose Tinted Glasses and the Fountain of Life

We had a one-on-one breakfast with Yossi at the Mercury Hotel in Koramangala, at my favourite table in a shady corner of the hotel garden.

Yossi didn't get enough sleep — he had arrived by my usual LH754 at 2:30 am. I didn't have much sleep either, so even my favourite masala omelette didn't appeal to me.

There was no point in beating around the bush.

"Yossi, you and Alex don't trust our numbers and don't give us a chance to explain. What do you want to achieve with this carpet bombing?"

"You're nice guys; even you, Vladi, sometimes, heh-heh. But your people have a problem — they are too positive. I don't want to hear about 'achievements' and 'accomplishments' even one more time. I am going to give your guys a beating, no matter what, until they stop being defensive and learn to look at reality without their rose-tinted glasses! And you too should decide which side you are on!"

Then Yossi's gaze shifted to something behind me, and his expression suddenly softened.

"Hey, Yossi, are you alright?"

He lowered his deep voice to a whisper, "Look, Vladi, what a beautiful girl!"

I was struck dumb — the fate of Evo was at stake. It was an issue of life and death, and my imposing boss was so easily distracted by a random girl? Reluctantly, I turned around and, pretending to look for a waiter, threw a glance at the table behind me.

Holy guacamole... I couldn't see the "beauty" Yossi had seen. How thick was the layer of rose-coloured tint on Yossi's glasses?

Yossi adored beauty in every form, whether it was software, art, or ladies. That's why he was so much in love with his beautiful French wife, who managed their family much more wisely than her husband managed his three-thousand-strong army of engineers, in my humble opinion.

Still, noticing some earthly beauty when Evo's fate was at stake was beyond my comprehension.

I looked at the girl again.

Hmm...

Maybe I was so stuck on Evo that I could no longer see the beauty around me? What if I'd misread Yossi? I saw him as a punisher, but maybe he had other things on his mind... women included?

Manoj told me once that in a bitter Buddhist hell, people mistake their loved ones for enemies that are attacking them. They start defending themselves with all sorts of weapons, killing left, right, and centre — until the veil lifts off their eyes, and they see themselves surrounded by the bodies of their loved ones whom they've just murdered.

And then the story repeats itself.

What if the purpose of Yossi's life was not to torment us? What if he was trying to help us, using unconventional methods? Harsh but effective ones — well tested already by the Spanish Inquisition.

The dense, fleshy leaves of the trees, covered with uneven layers of dust, longed for rain. Huge scarlet fish lazily moved their fins, as if half-frozen, in a narrow channel right under our feet.

I turned around again — and realized what Yossi had seen: the girl was not "beautiful," formally speaking. Not a Miss Universe contender. But she was charming, elegant, and glowing from within, as if a Fountain of Life was gushing through her.

Maybe, to see reality, you needed to wear glasses — sometimes rose-tinted, other times dark shades.

After finishing her breakfast, the girl got up and left, beaming with happiness and chirping on her mobile.

As my guru, Manoj, said, all good things in life either are not good for you, make you fat, or are already married to someone else.

Gurus and Inquisitors

Once in a small Tamil Nadu village, I watched with horror and disgusted curiosity as three half-naked men flogged themselves ardently and rhythmically. Blood dripped to the ground from their lacerated bodies, but they went on whipping themselves in a semi-trance. It was a religious ceremony of self-flagellation. A way to atone for guilt and please the gods.

This is how we started our journey of repentance and radical self-criticism, on the path laid out by Yossi and Alex.

Yossi wanted to teach us "critical thinking." According to Wikipedia — my guide to the galaxy — "Critical thinking is self-directed... and self-corrective."

We had to put aside the traditional Indian optimism and focus on the empty half of the glass and the dark side of the moon.

In the past, we used to say, "Yeah, we are late, as the STB drivers release from Korea was delayed. And our Israeli project manager didn't get the requirements right. But still, working hard, we have managed to reduce the delay to three months only!"

Now, having learned from Alex, we changed our style and put on the darkest glasses possible, "We are so sorry that the project is late again. We could have mitigated the risk of late STB drivers release had we written a simulator in advance. We should have sent our architect to capture requirements, not relying on others. But we will learn from our mistakes."

What we say affects how we think. Changing their language, my mega-positive Indian engineers got inoculated with Western "negativism." It hurt a lot. People in India do wash their linen in public but only literally, not figuratively. Things have to be kept in the family. Even in the West, very few organizations can admit to their screwups and lose face in public. Even a personal apology is easier than an organizational one.

"They say that the true guru is not the one who pleases your ego, but the one who breaks it. In this sense, Yossi and Alex are true gurus. They've forced us to get better — through pain." I shared my thoughts with Manoj.

"You'd be surprised, Vladi, but there are more gentle ways. Pain is not the only path to awareness," Manoj replied with a smile. "When we realize it, suffering ends."

From his lips to God's (and Yossi's) ears. We did realize there was another way — but not until a sizable pool of our blood gathered on the corporate floor. Then the beating stopped.

We were ready to move on.

Through Hardships to the Stars

We started the "Continuous Improvement Program" designed by Alex. Nothing in the corporate world is taken seriously without an acronym, so we called it "CIP."

Like a huge telescope dish aiming at a distant galaxy, our "system" began to turn in the direction of quality. People started to realize that quality is not about the number of bugs but the excellence of everything we were doing — from requirements to architecture to code to emails to the food at our canteen.

Quality is not in "how" we write code and test but in "why" we do what we do. In other words, quality is in engineering self-awareness.

Each quarter, teams reviewed previous outcomes and set goals for the next quarter — all by themselves. Then they presented to our top management. Each goal had to have metrics so that we could measure it.

People had figured out by themselves what no manager could convince them of: "good enough" was neither good nor enough. Massive code refactoring (gradual improvement) started. Murali, Evo's chief architect, spent nights debugging code with the developers, occasionally shouting at them.

Previously, our people were too busy to learn. We had to tie them to chairs in order to pour the wisdom of test-driven development, design patterns, and the intricate secrets of the English language into their ears. Alas, the wisdom went in one engineering ear and out the other.

CIP had brought personal motivation. "Don't want to learn? No problem! See you at the next quarterly review." That way, engineers started asking for courses. Education was turning from push to pull mode. We created conditions for the flow.

Our metrics were improving, and reality was catching up with the numbers. About six months later, Yossi started praising India on global forums. Not because we were so good but because others were worse. We went through the alchemical process of "sublimation," turning humiliation into humility, and humility into improvement. But in London, Paris, and Jerusalem, engineers still tried to rebel against the ferociously efficient "transformation by humiliation."

Yossi and Alex, the Eye of Sauron, fought those rebels, but they could not win the guerrilla war by carpet bombing. So they asked Shalini to help them with her magical people skills. This was the first truly global role for one of my employees. Starting out as Shalini's nightmare, metrics became her first step to the global podium.

Alex accepted my invitation for a drink. We were friends again, as India was the only site to adopt his baby, CIP, and to make it work.

Old People's Dances

Ron, our CEO, invited Manoj and me to the Executive Committee — an exclusive global club of top MCR managers from different sites, meeting once a quarter. Ron chose venues to his taste; no wonder they were always awesome.

Once, we met in Israel, at Timna — an amazing nature park by the Dead Sea. The secluded place looked like a giant abandoned construction site from the time of creation. Enormous ancient rocks of bizarre forms and shapes — building blocks of biblical giants, Nephilim, and dinosaurs — had been scattered here long before we came into being and would remain there long after us.

We rented the park for the night, and we were the only guests there. The five-star dinner was served in a sandy area between magnificent, wrinkled rocks that looked like the insides of giant elephant ears, under a starry sky that we could almost touch with our fingertips.

After the exquisite dinner, Ron's traditional sarcastic and witty speech was met with traditional well-deserved laughter and applause. A live band started playing. The members of the Executive Committee, mostly in their fifties and sixties, started dancing. Yirmi, our ever-young seventy-something VP of Security continued his wild dance on our makeshift dinner table.

The table collapsed — but in a leap on the verge of levitation, Yirmi kept his balance.

I've never seen Manoj so emotional.

"Vladi, this is so new to me... In India, when we grow old, we should not drink or dance — we should lead a spiritual life! But here... all this dancing... Yirmi is in a better shape than I am, at half his age!"

Manoj was serious about his yoga, but he was no match for Yirmi — a mountaineer, rock climber, and master of obscure martial arts.

Ageing fascinated me, as I was not getting younger day by day, and my Evo was not getting younger either. I felt terribly proud of my native West, which was so good at ageing.

The starry sky was slowly rotating above our heads. In India they say, "old is gold." Could we refactor ageing like we refactor software, getting better over the years?

Next day, as I was struggling with hangover during our boring corporate meetings, it occurred to me that wisdom, readiness for death, and calm are the competitive advantages of the elderly in India over the young. We — the elderly in the West — have lost them. So we dance on tables and chase our fleeting youth on the treadmill of life.

PART III. EVO AND THE RETIREMENT HOME

The Fly in the Ointment

While productizing Evo, we kept growing. One day we realized that Evo had already moved to the higher league, with fifty million end-users. They were like a virtual state, smaller than our Karnataka, but bigger than Spain.

Success, as we all know, is riskier than failure. While we dealt with small, peripheral customers, Neo leaders did not pay much attention to us. Now that we'd grown up, corporate aces noticed us. Not as a competitor but a nuisance. A random wrinkle in a perfect strategy, a fly in the ointment.

This had to be resolved. Neo managers kept insisting to our Sales, to Evo customers, and to Evo teams that a new product — superior in all respects — was almost ready, so the days of Evo were numbered. They expected Ron and Yossi to announce the date of Evo's funeral during their visit to India in a couple of weeks.

If Evo was no more, I would probably lose my job. But I had a plan. First, I could always sell my collection of Lufthansa pens that I'd gathered on my many flights. Second, I would compete with two pragmatic Russian girls: they worked in Bangalore as paid guests at local weddings. The presence of foreigners, even strangers, at family celebrations is prestigious and auspicious in India. The girls were somewhat prettier than me, but rank would be my competitive edge.

Anyway, that was plan "B." Plan "A" was to have a harsh conversation with my bosses. For too long, we'd been criticized for our "backward" Indian management, lack of innovation, questionable architecture, and low code quality. We'd listened, and we'd accepted, trying to improve. But Evo's "disadvantages" were the aces up our sleeve!

Long live the Tyranny!

Let's start with management.

Traditional Indian management style was indeed hierarchical and authoritarian, reflecting local socio-economic realities. Not just my favourite bureaucrat from the Mysore Palace — our very own chief architect, Murali, sometimes raised his voice, irritated with developers. He admitted this problem and sincerely wanted to improve. We talked, prepared improvement plans —and repeated the same conversation the next year.

Murali was not the only authoritarian; my decisions had not been put to a vote either.

Multipolar Neo management was very different, with all three main MCR centres equally and democratically represented. Three of Neo's chief architects — one in Paris, one in London, and one in Jerusalem — worked together, looking for the best solutions.

To each of them, the "best solutions" were his own. Not just personal egos were at play — architects stood up for their countries! National pride and the fate of battalions of developers were at stake.

Eventually, the architects compromised. But these compromises reflected current balances of political power in the organization, rather than an ideal architecture. This is how politics rules technology. Neo microservices were defined in accordance with the interests of and relationships between various groups. Component boundaries followed the political world map. With the arrival of a stronger leader in the UK, the architecture tilted towards the British side of the English Channel. And when the star of Israel rose in the corporate sky, the "conditional access" components from Jerusalem became central to the system's architecture.

Neo's organizational structure poorly impacted its architecture and obviously interfered with the delivery flow. The dreadnought of Neo was slowly moving forward — not due to its "democratic" and "multipolar" structure, but despite it.

Evo had just one chief architect, not as polished or brilliant as the Neo triumvirate. But our chances were in our shortcomings: unfashionably authoritarian, we were faster than the Neo perfection built around political compromises.

Neo management was proud that the best MCR talents from different countries (including my own Indian centre) worked together to make the Neo dream come true. Cooperation is wonderful, except that behind its façade, the Hundred Years' War was still flickering between the French, the Brits, and the Israelis. Some issues were minefields. Grenades were thrown in daily conference calls. Copying Ron on a ballistic email was like equipping it with a nuclear warhead.

We at Evo, on the other hand, were a large, messy Indian family sharing one house. Real people become outdated and go out of fashion these days, but we were not abstract online "resources." Our guys and gals went to the cafeteria together to eat generously salted and peppered watermelons. They played ping-pong on our roof, gossiped and fought, went to parties, and laughed together. And they dated each other, too: we already had more than a dozen internal weddings! Our people believed in our long-term success so much that one newlywed couple publicly committed to give birth to a developer or two for Evo.

Wires on Horns

We were often accused, "You don't come up with anything new of your own. You are just following Neo!" In a sense, we did — Neo paved the way. They had budgets for innovation and the best talent. How could we keep up with them?

And should we? After all, we followed so fast that sometimes we were ahead of our leader.

If something doesn't work in India, be it a water tap or a spacecraft, some "jugaad" is always found. A jugaad, or hack, is the easiest, fastest, and cheapest way to solve the problem without worrying too much about rules, quality, or aesthetics.

Instead of digging trenches for electric cables, it is easier to put them above. The thick web of electric wires in India is hung on trees, on poles, and on the horns of sad and wise sacred cows.

The jugaad, dirt-cheap bizarre-looking autos, built in Indian villages by local Fords and Edisons, cost a fraction of real cars. They are powered by cheap engines made from irrigation pumps sold at government-subsidized prices.

They say an Indian jugaad mission to Mars (2013) cost one-tenth of what NASA spent (less than a half by other sources, but still an achievement).

Western companies, including MCR, cultivate innovation in greenhouses, generously fertilizing it with money, under the tender rays of corporate bosses' attention. At international exhibitions, MCR's customers were taken to a cosy secret room where engineers from Neo's new initiatives unit showed them the future of television. Still, this future, like the horizon, always remains in the future — none of these amazing inventions have ever been deployed.

So do innovations need special conditions and the magical pixie dust of lavish budgets?

They say a woman once lifted a truck with her bare hands to save her child who was stuck under it. When they weighed the truck, it turned out that the woman had broken the world record for powerlifting.

Prisoners trying to escape are more innovative and resourceful than their guards. The prisoners' lives are at stake, unlike the guards'.

People become the most innovative in situations of scarcity and existential threat. Scarcity is in abundance in India; that's why India is so innovative — in its own unique way.

Our Evo lived under continuous existential threat, adapting and dodging all the time. But even in fairy tales, death can only be deceived for a while. The skeletal fellow with the scythe always has the last laugh. Not so long ago, the company decided that a new feature — recording TV programs from multiple rooms

— would be exclusive to Neo. We were not allowed to develop it. Evo customers who needed this feature would be forced to migrate to the new platform.

Besides, Neo people said, the cost of developing this functionality under the outdated Evo architecture was too high. Was it really? Murali, our chief architect, came up with a jugaad, tricking Linux into doing most of the work for us. Our colleagues from Neo didn't like it at all. It was an ugly hack of an operating system, not the generic, elegant solution that Neo engineers had been meticulously working on for the last year. Still, Murali's jugaad could save us sixty man-years; even with a late start, we could beat Neo to the market.

Let the brilliant Neo-lithians look down on our "so-so" engineers. My guys did not play with code for intellectual pleasure. Their passion was not perfection but practical outcomes. Not the eternal splendour of the code but the fleeting smile of the client.

In theory, there is no contradiction. The better the code, the wider the smile. In reality, perfection is worse than a hack: a hack can be quickly tested and corrected, but perfection, which requires eternity to achieve, cannot.

Would Ron and Yossi allow us to use Murali's jugaad?

And would they finally give me a budget for innovation? I'd been asking them for the last three years!

Old is Gold

The family row between Neo and Evo was a dispute between the "new" and the "old" generations of software. The main advantage of Neo was — it was newer.

When I first came to India, I thought maintenance was the last link in the development food chain. Maintaining a legacy product in a software nursing home was terminally boring.

I'm from the West, and the ageing West is obsessed with novelty and youth. "Old" in the West means falling into decay, degrading. The West, withering away, has not learned to grow old gracefully and accept its age. We even don't call people "old," using all sorts of euphemisms so as not to "offend" them.

Young India is very different — it respects and honours old age.

Most computer wallpapers across the globe are similar: if not kids, then romantic partners, or some glamorously photoshopped landscapes. But in India I saw pictures of elderly parents as computer wallpaper. Indian engineers and doctors go back to India, leaving their prestigious jobs and career prospects in the US or the UK to take care of their ageing parents.

Once during my first years in Bangalore, I got knee pain from overtraining in the gym. The doctor looked at all the test results, gave his recommendations, and then muttered somewhat apologetically, "Don't expect too much from your treatment, sir."

"Why not, doctor?"

"It's about age. You're getting old."

"Doctor, what are you talking about? I'm only forty-five!"

"Yes, that's what I mean. Forty-five — you're quite old, aren't you?"

I was a little upset, but Manoj explained that the doctor had done me a favour by lifting me early to the most respected age group. Being "old" in India is more respectable than being young. Important decisions, even the most sensitive, are made by seniors. Even most marriages in India are arranged by parents. Children recognize that more experienced parents can make better life choices for them.

Where does this trust in age come from? If we learn from experience, we become both wiser and better over time. And more adaptive, too.

Engineers refactor their code, gradually improving its quality. We applied the same practices to gradual improvement of architecture and technology, moving from C to Java, and from Java to JavaScript over time. That way, Evo evolved with age, getting better and better, while most other software systems degrade as they age.

This was what I would tell Ron.

Neo saw Evo as an old and rather annoying relative. Evo was sent to a modest retirement home in Bangalore to live there quietly for a couple of years and then bite the dust. Neo expected to inherit both Evo's customers and "resources."

But in India, people take good care of their ageing parents. Therefore, they are in a better position to understand the value of proper support for outdated software systems. We turned our retirement home into a... rejuvenation clinic! Evo didn't just refuse to die — it refused to grow old. With age, it became younger and better. Even better than its hapless heir.

Traditional Indian "shortcomings" — the ability to work by the rules and follow the leaders, patience and jugaad — had become our advantages in the high art of software maintenance.

Old is gold, they say in India. Old software is gold, quite literally: it needs much less investment and brings steady revenues. Evo revenues were about three hundred million bucks a year (including security and other streams it enables) — at relatively low Indian costs.

"Crew, please prepare for landing," the captain announced.

My story was just a version of reality — a view of the silver lining from above the clouds. Yossi and Ron couldn't be fooled by stories; they knew our problems pretty well. Yet, a story is the meta-reality that organizes our everyday life. Reality follows after the story like a fish follows a fisherman's lure.

I looked out the window; the magic carpet of lights across the dark ground below was twinkling festively. The lights of Bangalore always remind me of a huge Christmas tree. The higher I am, the more beautiful Bangalore is.

Problems usually start when I get closer.

"Ladies and gentlemen, we have just landed in Bengaluru."

My Agni Theyyam show on corporate burning coals must go on.

Book I: Conclusion

Two weeks after I had landed in Bangalore, Yossi and Ron came over to India, as planned.

We presented our story supported by numbers. Forty-plus broadcasters servicing more than fifty million pay-TV subscribers around the globe. I asked for some space for Evo. Perhaps with small customers, where heavy Neo machinery would be an overkill.

Yossi smiled benevolently; Ron, ironically and sceptically. Anyway, I got more than I asked for — a ban on Murali's jugaad had been lifted. We were sentenced to life.

Neo leaders were convinced that had the company moved all Evo resources to Neo, they would already rule the market. I was sure Evo could become an undisputed market leader for a fraction of the money invested into Neo. I asked our brilliant CEO why he had kept both platforms. Ron looked at me with a smirking, merciful smile and purred calmly in his deep velvet voice, "Why? Because I like it that way, Vladi."

Maybe Neo and Evo needed each other, as our competition made both systems better.

Our team scaled up with our platform. Padma and Shalini were promoted from directors to local MCR India VPs, following Manoj, who got that promotion earlier.

Western engineers are often in a solid state. They are who they are; they believe they already deserve more, so they are not too keen to change after promotion.

My Indian engineers were gaseous, so to speak — they filled the entire volume of their new roles as quickly as gas. They respected hierarchy, so after each promotion, they believed that they had to forget old skills and learn new ones. So they were soon ready for another promotion.

As for me, survival rather than promotion was always on my mind. But my move to India had paid off — the flow was carrying me forward. I had travelled a thorny path from a developer to a global MCR VP, without ever thinking about a career. Now only the stars, senior VPs, and Ron himself were higher than me in the company.

I just had to spread out my brand-new vice-presidential peacock tail. In my annual day speech, I mentioned flexibility and adaptability. The structures that create flows. The rules that make us free. And the humility required for change. I talked about the wonderful Indian art of rejuvenating ageing software. And of course, I mentioned the wise Lord Ganesha working on his laptop. He brought together the "material" and the "spiritual," the "personal" and the "professional," into a single whole.

I forgot to mention the most important thing: in good

times and in bad times, we had fun. We grew up, laughing together. That way, we had created a laughing organization.

This time there were no bullock carts or elephants at our annual day. In the end, right before the traditional fireworks and disco, we launched Chinese sky lanterns with burning candles inside. Hundreds of tiny lights were gliding in the warm air higher and higher, dissolving in the warm starry skies. I couldn't help but think about our fate. These flickering, quivering lights were like our own souls leaving us and ascending into the unknown.

While I was indulging in sentimental sadness, reflecting on the end of a beautiful era and the futility of all things, the Chinese lanterns were carried away by the wind.

They almost set the whole of Bangalore on fire for a giant Agni Theyyam.

FLYING BOAT

Book II

PART I. CORPORATE FIEFDOMS & COMRADE CHE

Head Transplant

A few months passed. Anxiety was in the air — something was brewing; we just didn't know exactly what. Ron, our CEO, made MCR a cash cow; he milked this cow, squeezing it to the last drop. Then pumped up the cow full again, repeatedly taking us public and private — always at peak price. Rumours had it either Microsoft was buying us, or we were buying Microsoft. You could expect anything from Ron.

The rumours were close; it was announced that MCR was acquired by Leviathan Inc, one of the giant US technology companies. From a Wall Street perspective, it was a perfect deal, a mythical "1 + 1 = 3" equation of synergy. While Leviathan had an enormous scale, MCR brought recurring software revenues, deep expertise in security, a sticky business model, and market leadership in our domain. Still, we were disappointed; our cocky little MCR had become the corporate prey of some mythological animal.

Leviathan's legendary president, a world-famous business leader, addressed us, MCR employees. He said we should feel very proud, as he had paid about a million bucks for each one of us. Still, "paying for us" was not the same as "paying us." We would have been a bit more proud had we got this money.

One of our engineers in Bangalore was literally sobbing when he heard the news; he had recently resigned from the Indian division of Leviathan to join MCR. Next day after he'd joined, Leviathan bought MCR. You can't get away if Leviathan is your karma.

For us, the senior MCR management, the future was sparkling with bright opportunities. We were even invited to spend a week with our new president and his lieutenants in the sacred chambers of Leviathan's headquarters. We breathed the rarefied, diluted air of those dwellings. We saw neural circuits flashing in the giant brains of Leviathan and imagined ourselves as a part of these circuits. We were throbbing with hubris, hope, and ambition.

Then the honeymoon was over.

We thought we would be a small but nimble and very clever fish in a big pond. Instead, it turned out that we were a small, dumbfounded, and completely lost fish inside a very big fish.

The acquiring company decided to "deeply integrate" us. In other words, to digest MCR and its brand, making it an integral part of Leviathan's corporate body.

Integration had to start with decapitation. Ron was too much for the system to digest: too shrewd, too witty, and too unconventional. Leviathan people thought he was a tyrant; indeed, a benevolent tyrant he was. He called all the shots — but only after listening to all of the opinions. His decisions could even be challenged, as Ron enjoyed proving his intellectual superiority in any argument.

So the integration began with the amputation of our head; Ron was offered a murky advisory role somewhere at the top but far away from us. The new leader appointed to replace Ron was much younger, more athletic, and taller than Ron. He was a true Leviathanian in spirit. Compared to the silky smoothness of his communication, Ron's accent sounded outdated. Everyone (including Ron) had hopes that the new leader would be a success.

Indeed, he was up for a good start. Soon, the new leader decided to visit us in Bangalore. He was already on the flight to India, but he never made it to Bangalore, mysteriously disappearing into thin air. Later we heard he'd left the company.

Another leader took over — and after just a few weeks announced his resignation. And then another one. Lord Ganesha had his head cut off and replaced with an elephant's head only once. Within months after our acquisition, we had the head of the organization bitten off and replaced four times.

Ron had built MCR as his boutique company, tailor-made for himself, for his benevolent Ganesha-shaped body. It was a big throne to fill, and perfect gym-chiselled Leviathan leaders didn't fit onto this throne. Leviathan was proud of its austerity; even the president's private jet was accounted as economy class. But without Ron's politically incorrect quips and witticisms, without his expensive wine in Michelin-starred restaurants and first-class flights, the gears of our organization could hardly turn.

New Leviathan leaders replacing those who had replaced those who bought MCR had no clue about MCR business. They were puzzled why their president had paid a few billion dollars for Ron's sarcastic smile, which had already faded in the air, like that of the Cheshire Cat. Ron had already left Leviathan, as had my boss Yossi and many other MCR veterans.

Our relationship with customers was deteriorating. The issues were piling up, but there was no one for the customers to complain to; the new leaders replaced each other in a cheerful merry-go-round.

We were still the 800-pound gorilla in our market — a depressed gorilla in deep existential crisis.

The Boat is Stuck

The same thing that happened to the (former) MCR was happening to us at Evo.

Prior to the acquisition, we were successful — or so we thought. Troubles had slowly been ripening deep inside, hidden from the eye. Acquisition had put this growth on steroids. Customers felt that we had become confused, slow, and expensive.

Running an organization is like running up the down escalator. The world of our customers was changing much faster than we were. But we had no time for the customers; we were too busy with the integration between the stubborn, prickly culture of MCR and the rounded, politically correct culture of Leviathan. Integration was sucking out our juices. In good times, the uncertainty of the future did not bother us; when in trouble, everyone was so concerned about the future that no one lived in the present continuous.

My people didn't enjoy their work anymore. Confused about uncertainties and grumbling about our corporate "system," they began to fall into a lethargic sleep of protest. Barnacles grew on the Evo ship and slowed it down. She was getting trapped in corporate mud.

A couple months ago, Padma told me, "We feel stuck, Vladi; please help us start moving again!" I wish I could.

A Russian friend sent me a meme.

> "Mom, I don't want to go to school! Kids laugh at me; teachers hate me!"

"You must go, darling. You have no choice: you are the principal."

Spot on.

So I went to school for countless conference calls and meetings. I grinded the Leviathan abbreviations. At MCR, we used three-letter project codes, but huge Leviathan used six-letter acronyms, thousands and thousands of them. We had to learn them by heart to be accepted.

I once read about the ancient Gnostic practice of memorizing the secret names of evil angels: a soul ascending to a heavenly abode can slip past an angel only if it knows its name. When the time comes for my soul to ascend, it will be saved by Leviathan abbreviations — they sound like the names of evil spirits. But at present, I couldn't cast a spell on them.

It is always darkest before the dawn. When we were on the verge of despair, a true angel unexpectedly descended into our vale of sorrow. It was Sandra — our brilliant new leader number five.

Sandra and the Orchid Powered Boat

Fifth time's the charm. If anyone could break the "MCR curse," it was Sandra. She was mega-smart, super-positive, hyper-optimistic, and uber-charismatic. Sandra was as polished and smooth in her communication as the surface of a brand-new car. She talked as if she was continuously presenting an invisible PowerPoint to the stunned and speechless Universe.

I admired Sandra's immaculate authenticity that was so well thought through. I was confident we would work well together — she was the one who could truly appreciate my Indian story!

Our business was still growing, so Evo's thousand-odd engineers were already stretched too thin. I had prepared a beautiful PowerPoint deck for our meeting with Sandra in California, asking her to approve 85 more engineers for Evo.

Sandra also came prepared for the meeting. Instead of wasting time on my slides, she got straight to business, "Vladi, Evo's profitability falls short of my expectations. You must cut your costs by a third; otherwise, I'm afraid your program will have to be closed."

Sandra's surgical smile was so charming that it took me a while to realize — "cutting costs by a third" meant laying off a third of my team. Not firing, of course, but right-sizing, as they said at Leviathan.

Goodness gracious.... To cope with the growth of business, a team reduced by a third must become twice as efficient. I had been in this business for many years, and I knew that this was utterly unrealistic.

I was gasping for air; instead of adding people, I had to let my guys go? And most probably, I would be "right-sized" as well.

Anyway, there was nothing to debate. Sandra had already sealed our short but entertaining meeting with the most dazzling of smiles.

This feeling of complete helplessness was sickening — the verdict had been rendered. Who cared if it was fair or not? With a feeling of dreary impotence, I had to take the flight to India and break the news to the team.

And then — thank God — on my LH754 from Frankfurt to Bangalore, I was upgraded to "business." There, in my cosy habitat, after the fourth glass of wonderful German Riesling, I had a strange dream. One of those you want to remember forever but can't recall even a few minutes after waking up, so I wrote it down:

> I am at the helm of a snow-white sailing ship, going up a wide, calm river across a pastoral landscape.

> Only instead of sails, the masts of my boat are blooming with huge colourful orchid flowers; their petals are slowly rotating. I realize that both the colours and slow silent rotation of the majestic petals make the ship glide upstream so easily, against the current, and a warm breeze is gently caressing my face.

Churches and villages and green pastures are replacing each other faster and faster; the river is winding more and more — until I suddenly realize that my white boat is flying above the surface of the water, effortlessly and smoothly. We are going faster and faster, higher and higher up as if dissolving in the blue tenderness of the skies.

Such a Disney-like sailing dream at my ripe age, funny me. I am so prone to seasickness I get it even in a bathtub. So why boats? On the other hand, there are real pirates in my lineage. The Jewish pirates of the Caribbean in the 16th century were direct descendants of rabbi Don Itzhak Abarbanel — a great doctor and a scholar of Kabbalah. I am his descendant too.

Even if the dream was just some rubbish, randomly tossed up by my subconsciousness, it smelled of fresh mint. Like hope or new love.

There is no better reason to change your life than a death sentence. Had it not been Sandra's corporate guillotine, Evo would have been drowning slowly and sleepily, like a ship's wreckage, for years. Now, thinking of a shiny, Dior corporate blade, I felt a prickle in my neck and electricity in my fingertips.

The death sentence liberated me. Maybe we could still turn Evo into the flying boat of my dream.

To talk the situation over with my team, I called an urgent meeting at the Coconut Grove resort in the suburbs of Bangalore.

From Bellandur with Love

It was early morning. Rajesh the driver had just picked me up from my new apartment at Bellandur, near the Outer Ring Road. On the bumpy way to Coconut Grove, I had been tossed about like James Bond's martini (shaken, not stirred).

How did I end up in the district of Bellandur?

After seven years of growth, MCR India had spread across five different offices in Koramangala. People from different offices were becoming strangers to each other, so it was high time to get together in one building.

Due to centripetal forces striving for unity, we were exposed to centrifugal forces. They threw us out of the shady but pricey paradise of Koramangala into the smelly industrial armpit of the Outer Ring Road. Now we were spread across three huge floors of a corporate building.

Space consolidation saved us money but had not entirely dismantled corporate borders; now, citizens of one floor looked with suspicion at foreigners from another floor.

Whenever our office moved, I followed and rented an apartment nearby to avoid the ridiculous Bangalore traffic jams. This time, I had dramatically downsized, choosing a modest-sized middle-class flat in the Exotica Prestige apartment complex.

I was the only foreigner in the building, quite comfortable in the very middle of middle-class habitat, in the most highly populated middle of nowhere in the Milky Way. I lived very close to our new office, just across the road. But I couldn't cross the expanse, unable to manoeuvre among the endless buzzing swarm of cars, even by hiding behind the local pedestrians. Rajesh the driver still picked me up every day, so every day I was stuck in epic traffic jams — ten minutes' walk from my house.

Every morning I slipped through gangs of monkeys on my way from the apartment to the parking lot in the basement. Monkeys roamed the corridors of Exotica Prestige, socializing, policing, checking out food in my neighbours' fridges, drinking their wine, almost smoking their cigars. It was not robbery — fully aware of their semi-divine status, the monkeys came to collect their due, self-assured and aggressively indifferent to humble humans, like tax collectors.

A neighbour told me that when the doorbell rang in the morning, she thought her husband had come back to pick up the car keys he had left behind. But when she opened the door, three grinning insolent monkeys were facing her. It's good they rang the bell; usually, they entered without warning, through a window, and went straight to the refrigerator.

This was the "memorandum" stuck on our announcement board, verbatim:

Primate menace: the Do's and Don'ts

- Keep your windows open with fine mesh to prevent the Primates from entering.

- Feeding Primates by animal lovers / religious minded people should be discouraged.

- Lock your fridge during the Primate visiting hours.

- Do not show your teeth to the Primate, you are challenging the Primate.

- Do not run away from Primates. As they know you are not its food, the Primates just want to socialize.

- Stand still if a Primate sits on your head, he will clear your hairs of lice.

The last point was irrelevant to me, as I had nothing left on my head to be cleared of lice.

We were approaching the hotel along a bumpy, countryside road. A driver of a colourful TATA lorry made a wavy hand gesture to Rajesh — "pass on, take over, the road ahead is clear." Blinkers were much less reliable or expressive than a friendly hand in the car window. So local drivers used a special gesture language. The world was changing — modern Indian Volvo buses had stickers saying, "No hand signals."

To discuss my revolutionary plans, I needed this offsite at Coconut Grove far away from the usual office setup — not just to "brainstorm" but to read my people's body language and hand signals. Who was going to support me? Who would get stuck? Who would overtake whom?

A Journey on the *Titanic*

It was a typical resort in the outskirts of Bangalore, all peace and quiet, shanti shanti green, with a swimming pool shaped like a huge Rorschach inkblot or a coffee stain and cute shabby cottages. Omnipresent and omni-impotent staff with permanently glued smiles were as accommodating as they were useless.

I invited just five people:

Manoj, my second-in-line, looking after the project management office (PMO), integration and testing, was having a last smoke before the meeting. Vijay, reporting to Manoj as a manager of his hundred-odd integration line, was chatting with him. Vijay was from Bangalore; he worked for ten years in Holland until his in-laws in Bangalore required help and care. Then, he and his wife had to return. I grabbed him upon arrival, almost on the plane, and brought him to MCR.

Shalini, in charge of our quality assurance and processes, and our chief architect, Murali, were already inside. Padma, looking after most of the Evo component development, hadn't arrived yet.

I entered a windowless conference room, saturated with the corporate boredom of endless meetings. Off-white walls, off-white boards, and an off-white tablecloth that had already passed its prime. Battered chairs still remembered the long-gone scarlet glamour of their youth. What a mundane and dull backdrop for our dramatic offsite....

Padma was rushing into the room, slightly out of breath, with a guilty and concerned smile — am I late?

You are forgiven, Padma.

We didn't need an icebreaker; an account of our nice chat with Sandra would break any ice....

People were listening in tense silence.

"How come we have become less profitable overnight, Vladi?" asked Padma.

Indeed, we'd always thought we are as profitable as a money printing press. I explained:

"The gears of accounting machines turn slowly. They have just started charging us in India with G&A (global and administrative) expenses of the mothership in California. It doesn't make much sense, but rules are rules, you know."

Besides, our "revenue attribution" was a mess: Evo was sold as a part of a bigger package. Some offerings, like conditional access, were priced highly. Others, like Evo, were given away for peanuts. This pricing was artificial; customers cared about the whole end-to-end package. Without Evo, no one would pay for conditional access.

"What does Sandra think about it?"

"She doesn't think anything about it — she is not interested in such minor details. I tried to explain it to her while we shared a ride to the airport, but she was chatting to her friend on the phone and kindly asked me not to waste oxygen on this topic. No point in trying again — if we are marked as 'defensive,' we are dead."

In fact, we were dead anyway. If we reduced head-count, we would not be able to cope with the amount of work. If we argued, they'd shut us down immediately.

Silence.

"How much time do we have, actually?" enquired Murali gloomily.

"Not too much. Sandra said we must finish cost reductions within a year. But I am sure she is not going to wait. We have to show her something tangible in four or five months."

"It is too little time, Vladi. And expectations are too high."

Murali was right. Every organization, even the most efficient one, gains some flab during its years of plenty. To improve by ten or even fifteen percent, we could cut some flab, do some pep talking, let a few people go... We could have "Bangalored" a few jobs, had we not been in Bangalore.

But we couldn't become twice as productive by squeezing dry the current way of working. — And it was our chance!

"Think of it this way." I picked up this expression from Padma and couldn't get rid of it. "In the past, Ron, Yossi, Alex, and other moms and pops from the headquarters decided how we had to work. Sandra doesn't care about the 'how,' just the 'what' — the end goal. In the meantime, we are flying under her radar. So we can use this cost reduction exercise to completely redesign Evo. Like, radically."

I would not say my people were overwhelmed with enthusiasm. Anyway, I kept going.

"Let's accept the inevitability of death, oh my corporate brethren and sistren, and become free. Thanks to Sandra, we have nothing to lose. In the worst case, we will add a few lines about transformation experiences to our boring resumes. The plan is simple — just change the paradigm!"

Cannons vs Missiles

"Paradigm shift" sounded encouraging — if only we knew what our current paradigm was, what our future paradigm would be, and how to shift. We had to go over it point by point, starting from the current paradigm.

Like everyone these days, we were adaptive, fast, and "agile" in our spirit. As to the flesh of our operating model, it was sinful — we worked in a good old waterfall process.

Actually, the term "waterfall" sounded outdated and vulgar in a refined Leviathan environment. Instead, we said, we work in a "predictive paradigm." It assumed that we could predict and plan everything in advance. If we took all factors and risks into account and aimed our Big "Predictive" Cannon right, we hit our target — delivery of useful features.

Predictive Cannon shoots well — if both its target and the Cannon itself stay in place.

But our targets — business requirements — were changing faster and faster. Oddly enough, sometimes our releases were late upon arrival, even when they were on time. While we were working on a big project, market conditions changed.

A cannon is a poor choice for shooting at moving targets. To hit a moving target, we needed....

"A self-guided missile!"

"Thank you, Vijay! Exactly! Such a missile keeps checking its own location and the target's location, adjusting its course to the target's movements."

Not just business requirements change. Technologies

fall from grace, and new ones emerge. Our team was in flux — people came and went. Even managers' moods changed, and that matters — ask Padma's team, heh-heh. We had just been acquired; who knows what would happen tomorrow — a pandemic, a discovery of the immortality pill, or an alien invasion...

This was the essence of the adaptive paradigm: be aware of your market, your ecosystem, and your team. Release as often as you can. Ask for feedback: "Have we delivered useful features? Is our quality good?" And course-correct fast.

"How often do you think we should release?"

"As often as we can, Manoj. Maybe once every couple of weeks to start with?"

Manoj was smiling compassionately as if I'd just cracked a Russian joke that no one in my foreign audience could understand:

"Vladi, it would be just wonderful! The catch is, our customers would never deploy that often, you know — it is costly over satellite. Two weeks? I would be surprised if they deploy once a quarter!"

"Well, customers can play with our releases and give us feedback, even without deploying them to end-users. Customers can change things. We adjust. Repeat forever. Ta-dah!"

"Wise guys like Alex and Martin Fowler say, the more often we release, the smaller the number of changes, and the easier it is to test the system — so the quality improves," Vijay suggested.

"Mmm... Right.... Working software every two weeks... Just two issues, Vladi-ji," Manoj addresses me as a senior, almost with embarrassment. "First, we will become slower and more expensive: each release requires a cycle of integration and testing. The more releases, the more cycles, so we'll have to hire a hundred people more, I am telling you!"

"Anything else?"

"And second, let's not fool ourselves. Releasing once in two weeks is just not possible," Manoj nodded very convincingly to himself. "We are not in the cloud."

Why was it "not possible"? Due to a whole bunch of problems, but first of all, integration.

Component Teams and Integration Hell

Customers said they would put up with our delays if they knew how late we were going to be. We were always on time until we entered the integration valley of death. Then no one knew when we would cross it — integration is slow, painful, and unpredictable.

Let's see why.

Tens of millions of lines of Evo code were organized into software components and layers. Each of Padma's development teams owned a component or a few. Only a team that owned a component could modify its source code.

Ownership is good, isn't it? But here is the catch. For every end-to-end feature, we had to change code across multiple components. That way, every feature had to be decomposed into tasks for each team. Project managers brought a dozen of the component owners together to make them agree on the division of work.

But each component owner wanted to grab more — that's how they got more significance and weight in the system. Like feudal lords, component owners live off their code allotments. They defend their assets from other fiefdoms and wage turf wars to expand their own. The more work, the more subordinates; the more subordinates, the sooner a sweet promotion is coming.

After a few violent rounds (spiced up with some of Murali's trademark shouting), a feature was decomposed between teams, and development started.

When teams were on their own, they made good progress and finished development on time. Some components had to wait for others. Still, by no means could teams touch each other's code. Not just touch — even see. Some managers protected their code from indecent glances like a jealous husband hides his beautiful wife. What's behind the API façade was no one's business.

When all teams were finally done with development, integrators put updated components together. We were just like the municipalities in India. The annual monsoons catch them by complete surprise. We knew integration was coming, but something was always missing or mismatched. Side effects and nasty end-to-end bugs crept out of their hiding places.

End-to-end issues were always orphans; they hovered in between, on the seams, alongside organizational borderlines. Project managers helped the integrators, but component owners did not care about end-to-end problems. Let integrators deal with that headache. They were the ones getting paid for it!

Metrics Shape Reality

Component owners didn't care about end-to-end features and customers, but quality metrics were of their utmost concern. That's how managers are assessed and rewarded.

We were proud of our metrics; we measured everything we could on the component level, and our numbers kept improving. Alas, our relationships with customers did not.

Paul, a Western expat CTO of our big Indian customer, was quite expressive for an English gentleman:

"Vladi, your people show me all sorts of data to prove that your quality is improving. 'Our cyclomatic complexity has decreased by one and a half percent and blah-blah-blah.' I don't give a damn about your f*ckomatic complexity if you release the same crap!"

We think data reflects reality. Actually, data shapes reality: what we measure affects how we think and how we act! We were measuring the wrong numbers, so we did the wrong things. It was like playing bug ping-pong.

Testers wanted to report more defects to show better "numbers." Developers wanted fewer bugs reported — it ruined their quality metrics (and bonuses). They beat a bug off, back to testers — "No, it's not a bug!" Or, "This bug has already been reported under a different name!"

Other ping pong games started between component owners, each worried about their own metrics:

"It is not my bug — it is your bug!"

"Nope, it's yours!"

Lunch Break

We broke for lunch, stepping out of the cold conference room into the sparkling, twittering greenery of the garden. Nature in India has not yet decided what it will look like. It tries on one shape after another: flowers look like birds, birds look like flowers, women look like butterflies, and butterflies.... The butterflies fluttering around were as big as eagles and as bright as stained-glass windows in Indian churches.

"So far so good," as someone falling from the roof of the skyscraper says, flying by the eightieth floor.

Padma handled it pretty well — although her component owners had just been carpet-bombed, she seemed to enjoy the intellectual pleasure of bombing her own teams. Manoj looked content — we were dealing with the issue of Padma's component owners, which has been hushed-up for years.

We were heading for the open-air dining room with a typical lunch buffet in an Indian hotel, almost the same everywhere. Authentic homely Indian food is truly a treat, but the hotel food was too spicy, too oily, and too heavy for me.

Manoj had his "non-veg" day today. Padma was "pure veg," like Murali, but she sometimes drank wine. Shalini was "both veg and non-veg." This non-binary logic made sense — veg and non-veg are two distinct cuisines, not just dietary restrictions. Both Vijay and I ate anything without asking too many questions.

We filled our plates...

"Vladi, tell us honestly — why has Yossi left?"

"I have no clue, Padma — he would never tell me."

"Pleeeease, Vladiii...."

"Well, I don't know... I can only share rumours. They say a couple of our guys from the UK were given certain promises by Leviathan. Those promises were not kept, and Yossi interfered. It went up to Sandra. She told him, 'You know, Yossi, my team is so aligned that if I start a sentence, everyone on my team can finish it. I don't feel it the same way with you.' 'You want me to finish your sentences?' replied Yossi, astonished. And resigned the next day. Then he called me to say he was sorry he wouldn't be able to help us anymore. He sounded happy, though. Anyway, those are just rumours; no one knows for sure, and he would never tell — he is too good a corporate player."

Shalini and I were going for second servings of ice-cream. Padma was on some severe penance — she skipped dessert, which I knew she loved.

Shalini looked a bit sleepy. When her in-laws were visiting, like now, she had to get up at 5 am at the latest to cook for them. Even if a daughter-in-law is a high-ranking manager in an international company, she must personally cook for her in-laws daily — no maids or cooks. To do otherwise would be disrespectful.

"Why can't you just cook once and store it in the fridge?"

"Come on, if it is refrigerated, it is not 'food!' Nobody puts food in the fridge, especially when in-laws or parents are around."

"Why do you need a fridge, then?"

"For ingredients, Vladi...." Shalini stared at me almost pitifully, surprised by my naivety.

If we were being praised at all by Leviathan, it was for our "gender diversity": almost thirty percent of our engineers were female. Quite a few of them were successful managers.

I was happy to take credit for the gender diversity. Although I never thought of diversity when hiring or promoting people. Our ladies made it to the top because they were strong, technically sound, and courageous, not because of corporate campaigns. True diversity is when people think differently, regardless of their gender or looks. True equality is when no one even thinks about equality, so natural it is.

We hadn't run inclusivity campaigns either, but we did have differently abled people on board. They were good engineers; that's why they were with us.

We were not the garden of Eden, not at all. From time to time, I heard muffled grudging about the Tamil mafia or the Kerala clique at the office. Once I discovered an all-brahmin team, led — by pure coincidence — by a brahmin team lead. Still, with so many dimensions of diversity — education, language, religion, native place, caste, faith, food, cricket, politics, and gender — none of them were toxic. People easily bonded with each other across all these dimensions.

Padma looked at her watch:

"Guys, it is getting late; I don't want to pay a fine! Go, go, go!"

Shuffling the deck

Everyone was back on time, at 2 pm sharp. Typical for my team but quite exceptional for India.

As for me, I hate to keep others waiting, so I am never on time — I am always too early, even when I am trying my best to be late. I am afraid I will come too early even for a rendezvous with my angel of death.

We had an agreement with my team: whoever was late for a meeting paid a fine, which went into a communal piggy bank. But the bank was empty — my stingy teammates were always on time for my meetings and were comfortably late for meetings with their subordinates.

Back to business.

We believed that integration was a given, a fact of life. We'd tried to improve it over the years but without much success. In reality, the integration hell was of our own making. It was a direct outcome of our org structure!

We asked managers to cooperate, but we set up org structures and metrics for conflicting interests. We convinced people to work together, but we paid them for taking care of their fiefdoms first. We focused on end-to-end, but we measured local optimums of siloed teams.

How could we eliminate integration and focus development teams on end-to-end functionality?

"We've already been through this before, Vladi; we need to change our organizational structure," suggested Shalini.

The usually calm lake of Manoj's face rippled.

"This is too vague, Shalini. What do you mean?"

"Just give the teams ownership of end-to-end functionality instead of components. Then you don't need integration at all. That's what Craig Larman is talking about!"

Vijay shrugged. To him, it sounded too simple.

Craig Larman's brilliant article was recommended to us by Alex, our Jerusalem guru. Craig believes that teams should not be responsible for "components" (even if they are called "microservices" or "products") but for what is important to the client — end-to-end features.

For such "feature teams" to move quickly, they need autonomy. They should be allowed to change the code of any component all by themselves, without wasting time asking others and waiting for them. No private ownership of code — all of the code should be accessible to everyone!

Not only the code — teams should be able to do everything that is necessary to release a feature by themselves, including dealing with delivery pipelines and databases. Therefore, such teams have no one to fight with, no one to "cooperate" with, and no one to integrate the code with — they release end-to-end features by themselves!

This is pure magic. Autonomous lean and mean teams follow their customers like self-guided missiles: they receive feedback and course-correct. Such teams should be the building blocks of our future organization.

Checkmate. I rested my case.

Vijay smiled absent-mindedly at the Universe. Padma was vibrating with enthusiasm — she was always quick to sense new opportunities.

"Means, I take one engine guy, one UI guy, a couple of middleware guys, an integrator and a couple of testers, maybe one DevOps guy — and form one team!"

Uh-oh... with one elegant move, Padma had not just shuffled all her component teams — hundreds of engineers — but also taken over Vijay's integrators, who were ultimately Manoj's people. I thought Manoj would stand up for them. But he was struck by a different thunderbolt.

"Are you kidding me, Padma? Are you going to dismantle the infrastructure team? Then who will support the infra?"

Manoj looked at Vijay in surprise, as if asking for support. Manoj trusted his technical knowledge. Besides, Vijay did not just report to him; they were also friends.

"Padma is right. Everyone will take care of infra," Vijay almost purred with pleasure, like a cat after a heavy lunch.

"If we keep infra separate, others will have to integrate with it, and it will slow us down. Let's distribute the infra guys and integrators between feature teams so that teams can change infra all by themselves."

Oh, my God. Disbanding infrastructure teams was radical. But to avoid integration, dependence on infrastructure must be nipped in the bud.

Like all other dependencies.

Assembly Line or 3D Printer?

Manoj looked as if his teammates had suddenly turned into toddlers and he was the only adult in the room left to change their diapers.

"Vijay, what are you talking about? Just imagine the mess without ownership or personal responsibility for the code! Hundreds of developers tinker with the whole stack, including infra — at the same time. It's going to be a disaster!"

Manoj was right — the unattended code would be instantly polluted, like picnic spots on Nandi hills near Bangalore. But code ownership created corporate kingdoms and integration hell.

"Yep, the code must be controlled as well as the design. Let's introduce internal 'open source' with strict code moderation!" Vijay was on a roll. "Like the big boys, Linux or Mozilla, just for us."

This was not an improvisation. Vijay and I prepared for the meeting together and had a sweet argument about Craig Larman's articles.

With no support from Vijay, Manoj turned to me.

"Vladi, if we produced cars, would you like each team to build its own? Or would you build a conveyor belt — an assembly line where every type of work is performed by experts?" Manoj raised his eyebrows.

It was a good question. Instantly, Padma shot ahead of me.

"Think about it this way — functional teams are 3D printers; no need to assemble anything from parts — each team prints a whole car. This is the future of the automotive industry!"

"Not everything can be 3D printed," Manoj replied after a moment's hesitation. "Feature teams, like printers, are too small for large functionality!

Printers make toys, and it's not the same as printing a lorry."

Good point. But maybe we could slice functionality so thinly that each slice fits into a 3D printer!

Anyway, these were details. We'd figure them out later.

Let's get back to the organizational structure.

Corporate Che Guevara

"Each team develops a full end-to-end feature, so there is no need for integration. Thank you, Vijay, for your good work — your department can now be closed. Congratulations!" fired Padma with her trademark vicious smile.

Vijay nodded, smiling back at her. He didn't care if his team was dispersed. He'd do something else, something more interesting. Vijay didn't care about carrots and was not afraid of sticks; he didn't have attachments, which made him completely unmanageable. I didn't know if he was a Buddha or an anarchist. Most likely, he was both.

The next move was clear to me:

"With feature teams, we don't need to deconstruct features into tasks and distribute them between teams. There is also no need to integrate tasks. So, what is left for project managers to do?"

We stared at each other like partners in crime, getting ready for the bank robbery. The project office was the heart of our organization. Our best people traditionally flocked to Manoj to become project managers; this was the most respected job since they were the ones who assembled disparate components into one product.

But with autonomous teams, project managers do not need to "coordinate," beg people for "cooperation" or "focus on end-to-end features." Focus and cooperation were already woven into the very fabric of the adaptive organization!

"What are you talking about, Vladi? Do you mean we should disband the Integration department, Project management office, and Testing department?" Manoj was astounded.

"Yeah, I guess we'll have to. Otherwise, the old structures will interfere with the new methods of work. Integrators will be in high demand for autonomous teams — they are good coders, and they understand the structure of the entire system. Testers, too. But what do we do with project managers, for God's sake... We need to find them other roles."

It was kind of ironic that Manoj ran all these three departments — integrators, testers, and PMO.

Manoj also found it ironic, judging by the bewildered look on his face. I thought I had done some preliminary loosening of the soil by sending out a few articles by Craig Larman before the meeting. Apparently, no one expected me to take them so seriously.

Neither did I. But while I'd been preaching to my team, I had seen the light myself — and gotten carried away by the poignant pleasure of designing from a clean slate. I should have worded my message about project managers more softly. Still, the blood was throbbing in my temples — this was a revolution! Down with integration! Down with dependency on infrastructure! Down with the ownership of the code! We'd take it away from the component nobility and hand it over to the communes — our feature teams. Anyone could modify any piece of code!

Down with the project management office!

I felt like a corporate Che Guevara.

There was just one minor problem. Revolutions usually start with the best of intentions and end up in a bloody mess. Those "evil" component lords and project barons were our best people.

But thank God and thanks to Sandra — we had no choice.

Kabbalah and Teamwork

ItIt was getting late. I was exhausted, thrilled, and scared at the same time.

Time to recap and wind up.

Adaptive organization is based on feedback and rapid change. Therefore, we should release the code to customers as often as we can, not less than every two weeks.

We had to change the entire operating model: everything that could be formally described and drawn on the board — our structures, processes, frameworks.

In other words, we would blow up the whole edifice that we had built with loving care, brick by brick, over the years. We would scrap our component metrics that we created with Yossi in our glorious past and make everyone focus on a single goal: how to release faster.

We would scrap our process that we were so proud of. To get rid of integration, we would demolish our biggest teams, Manoj's crown jewels. That is, the project management office, integration department, and testing department, with hundreds of engineers in each.

We would ruin careers and hurt people. And in doing so, we would let every third engineer go.

"What an inspiring plan!" Padma chimed in.

I couldn't do it alone. I needed my team more than ever. Vijay was with me. So was Padma, despite her irony — they both loved the thrill and the crisp, fresh winds of change. They also loved fireworks, so they wouldn't mind a few explosions. Murali didn't care much; he was a technical guy, living entirely inside our codebase, like a worm in an apple. Shalini was thrilled but cautious, and that's good — it was her role to bring my spacecraft back to planet Earth.

The issue was with Manoj. He felt disoriented and betrayed; he didn't get it, why his best teams had suddenly become an obstacle on the way to some murky corporate Nirvana.

I felt for him. He was an excellent manager: delegating, caring, humble, and honest. He was deeply respected and liked by our people. Without his support, our ship would get stuck in the corporate mud. He held the keys to the kingdom.

I couldn't lose him — or anyone else, for God's sake... I wanted them to feel what I felt. I needed a story.

> It happened in the Middle Ages, in Spain. A profound scholar of Kabbalah, Rabbi Shimon, together with many other Jews, was persecuted by the Spanish Inquisition for following the Jewish faith. After days of torture, they were sentenced to be burnt alive. Until then, the Jews were placed in a prison cell together. Most of them started praying. Others tried scratching and cracking the stone floor and walls.

> Rabbi Shimon did not pray. Instead, he pierced his finger and started drawing on a cell's wall with his own blood — he drew a beautiful ship, sailing in the ocean. At midnight before the execution, the

painting was finished.

"Who is ready to sail with me?" asked the Rabbi.

No one replied, as they were all too busy — praying, sobbing, and crying. Rabbi Shimon kept asking again... and again.... But his fellow Jews thought he had lost his mind.

At the crack of dawn, when they could already hear the guards' voices in the corridor, Rabbi Shimon whispered a few words — and the painting on the wall came alive. People in the cell sensed the pungent smell of the sea and the salty breeze. This was the last and final call to board the ship...

I tweaked the original happy ending of the story.

Alone, Rabbi Shimon couldn't steer the big vessel in the stormy ocean; he would end up crashing on the rocks and dying.

But if his cellmates trust him, they will navigate the ship together, living beautiful lives full of adventures!

Back to our world. Our corporate Inquisition is after us, but we've already started drawing the new Evo ship on the whiteboard. The ending of the story is up to us. So let's make Evo into an impossible self-guided flying boat, for God's sake!

Ta-dah....

I exhaled. I admit, I'd gotten shamelessly carried away by the salty winds of this story.

"Wow, Vladi, you are getting so much better with motivational speeches... almost as good as Sandra," chuckled Padma. She was sarcastic as usual, but her huge dark eyes were glowing.

In software, stories and metaphors are as important as technologies and frameworks.

PART II. LEADERS & POLICEMEN

Corporate Phantoms

"Radical change? Adaptive organization? Flat hierarchy? In India? In less than a year? Oh, just a thousand-plus people! Sure, a piece of cake. Don't drink and drive, Vladi — smoke and fly!" Alex casually advised.

We (ex) Eastern Europeans believe that encouragement is for sissies. I actually loved Alex's advice, as I was drawing a flying Evo boat.

But the drawing could only happen after midnight, when I was already turning into a pumpkin: most of the day and the first half of the night were spent on the usual firefighting and "integration" — both technical and organizational integration of MCR India into the giant Leviathan body.

Leviathan swallowed companies in schools, like a sperm whale devours small fish. We were still at the very beginning of its long digestive tract, in the benevolent jaws of its highly professional integration team. We spent hours on conference calls discussing "getting aligned on coordination activities" and other equally exciting topics.

Conference calls also touched upon such mundane issues as mapping employees to the Leviathan job family and salary ranges. Some of my people got demoted, while others were unexpectedly promoted in accordance with the laws of corporate karma — the logic of which was above mere mortals' understanding. That way, Manoj was mapped to a Senior Director level — one step above Padma and Shalini, who both were downgraded from MCR regional VPs to plain vanilla directors. I tried to explain and fix it, but my standard corporate ammunition didn't work against friendly, professional, and smiley integration phantoms.

All their decisions were made collectively and anonymously, somewhere in the mysterious depths of the corporate guts. The verdicts that reached us were usually expressed in a passive voice: "it was decided that...." Who made the decision remained unknown. Dozens and dozens of highly paid specialists were involved in our integration, and there was no one to talk to.

I failed to persuade the Leviathan integration team to allow us to keep our perks — free fruit and lunches. Their cost for the whole year was negligible compared to the cost of hours spent on discussing them. And their value was tangible: quite a few people joined us just because they heard MCR was a crazy company giving out food.

If you take food away from engineers, they think that the company is going down, even if the price of its stock is going up. Both God and the devil are hiding in small things and details — having lost such a trifle as heartily peppered and salted watermelons, our engineers looked sorrowful. Even small salary increases did not raise their spirits.

We were out of time for planning the revolution — we just had to do it.

Process and Shamanism

At the Coconut Grove offsite, we — the Coconut team, as we called ourselves — admitted that to survive, Evo must become an adaptive organization composed of small autonomous teams. To get rid of integration hell, each team should release entire end-to-end features every two weeks.

Nice dream.

But how do such teams operate? Who does what, how, and when in such teams? And why?

The Evo process that we were so proud of answered all these questions.

Sadly, flexible in its youth, our process had passed the expiration date, become stale, and grown a capital letter "**P**" for itself. In the past, it stopped people from doing silly things. Now silly things were done in the name of the **P**rocess. "Has Murali already signed this document? Ah, not yet? Well, I'm not going to do anything until he signs!"

Why not replace the process with an Agile framework?

"Agile again?" smiled Shalini.

Exactly. A few years ago, we thought of moving to Agile, but at the time, I couldn't change the paradigm — or I thought I couldn't. Still, there was no litmus test for an "Agile mindset," so we declared our culture to be Agile!

Now our litmus test was fortnightly releases to customers. For that, we must change not only the spirit but also the letter of the operating model. Scrum was the most natural choice. Many companies had moved to it and seemed happy. Why should we reinvent the wheel when we have to invent a flying boat?

"Sure, Vladi. Scrum is the way to radically increase productivity! Only, Scrum Masters and Product Owners do not write code, so a quarter of a Scrum team is unproductive," said Padma in her sweetest and most innocent voice. "What did you call Scrum last time — black magic or Shamanism?"

Shamanism. But it was a different epoch. Then I could afford to "master" Scrum after reading a couple of articles and watching a video or two on the Web. Times have changed, and the stakes are too high.

"I need a deep dive into Scrum, Padma! The good news is — we all need it!"

The whole Coconut team signed up for Scrum Master and Product Owner certification courses. To speak the same language, we had to learn together.

Agile Jeans

The training was held in a hotel boardroom. This time the hotel was posh. Not just five stars, but a whole constellation of stars were twinkling on its signboard in the centre of Bangalore. Only in Asia do they know what true luxury is.

A world-class Agile expert — a British expat living in nearby Sri Lanka — clarified to us the mechanics of Scrum. Practices that were counterintuitive at first glance began to make sense.

At school, the best part of the lesson is the recess bell. Our courses were crisp, entertaining, and informative, but the tea and lunch breaks were even better. I love velvet-smooth Masala chai, which tastes like home. I also love fragrant, juicy Indian gossip.

I got plenty of both.

I was the only non-Indian, middle-aged senior manager in my classes. Other aspiring agilists were about half my age and at the bottom of the organizational pyramid. To make them feel more comfortable in my presence, I introduced myself as an Israeli leader of a small team just visiting Bangalore. It was true. I just didn't mention how many years ago my visit had started.

Feeling at ease around me, people talked. One girl, looking like a slim teenager, was especially chatty. "Our bosses think they understand Agile. But they expect real results from wearing Agile jeans!" she was chirping.

What? Jeans?

Yeah, here's the thing: during her company's "transformation," the CIO started coming to work in jeans instead of his usual formal suits to make a point about his conversion to Agile. Others followed. Every employee had received an Agile t-shirt and a DevOps cap. The air buzzed with motivational speeches.

But delivery pipelines were not automated, organizational structures and metrics were not changed, and no feature teams were formed.

Good old corporate kingdoms adopted the Agile mumbo-jumbo. The CIO's jeans were the only tangible outcome of their transformation.

Well, that was not bad — their CIO had at least bothered to change into "Agile jeans." Others simply delegated change to the QA department, the Project Management office, and such.

Woe and alas, old structures cannot be trusted to pull off a paradigm shift — they are part of the problem, not part of the solution. Their very existence is questionable in the new model. Tasking legacy teams with change is like asking corporate foxes to guard a henhouse.

In general, delegating transformation downstream sends a message to the whole organization: instead of changing yourself, ask your subordinates to change. This is what everyone does. Eventually the only ones who change are the "office boys," as they have no one to delegate to.

As for me, I would have happily delegated everything. But I couldn't afford this luxury, as my neck ached at the thought of Sandra and her guillotine.

Another participant, a cheeky, chubby young man, shared his story.

"Agile values, such as 'trust,' 'courage,' 'openness,' 'focus,' 'teamwork,' and such, were printed on all the walls of their office overnight. It was impossible to get away from them, even in the bathroom.

"Values were printed on the walls, and have remained there, not infiltrating the sceptical minds. Behaviours haven't changed at all.

"Actually, they have!" The young man corrected himself. "It's, like, 'trust' and 'openness' are in every sentence. Hypocrisy is booming."

I've heard enough — it's all about management. Top managers don't care much about the details, as they believe that the Universe grants them understanding, out of respect for their designations. When managers talk Agile, they mean the Holy Spirit of agility. When developers talk Agile, they mean the letter of the operating model — roles, responsibilities, practices, pipelines, and structures.

Most "transformations" fall in the crack between the letter and the spirit.

Curling (Non-)Management

TheThe coach talked so deliciously and beautifully about Scrum practices that we wanted to try them on guinea pigs. Besides, we had just passed exams to become Scrum Masters and Product Owners. A certificate always convinces its owner of the value of the knowledge obtained. So we decided that Scrum was the best operating model for feature teams.

There was, however, a lacuna in the course curriculum. I wanted the trainer to explain how Scrum teams are managed, but management issues were beyond the curriculum's scope.

What about the Scrum Masters and Product Owners we'd talked about so much? — No, they didn't "manage" the teams; they just played with them... curling!

When I first saw curling on the TV, I didn't get the point. As if a few janitors were frantically sweeping and scrubbing the ice floor, preparing for a sudden return of the Snow Queen.

That was not far from the truth.

According to Wikipedia, "Curling is a game played on ice, especially in Scotland and Canada, in which large, round, flat stones are slid across the surface toward a mark. Members of a team use brooms to sweep the surface of the ice in front of the stone's path, to control its speed and direction."

So do the Scrum Masters. They do not "manage," and they have no subordinates. They just help their teams glide faster by "polishing the ice" of their path. They protect teams from superiors' pressures. They eliminate any and all dependencies and obstacles that slow down their teams — from misunderstandings in requirements to the quality of the coffee. But release dates and delivery issues are not the Scrum Masters' concern. They are "servant leaders." Like doting mother hens, they take care of the teams, and the teams take care of the delivery.

The Product Owners' job is different — they work with the customers, clarifying their needs and relaying their feedback to the teams to better aim the "stone" at ever-changing requirements. No one on the teams reports to them, either.

In the traditional predictive model, managers decide

"what" the team does and "how" it does it. Scrum takes that away: the Product Owners decide "what" the team does. "How" things are done is defined by the Scrum model. Scrum Masters make sure this model is implemented properly.

In Scrum, there are no managers at the delivery steering wheel — teams, like self-driving cars, manage themselves. A friend recently invited me to check out a self-driving car developed by his company. It was startling. The car drove fast along a fenced road, turned and bypassed objects — while the driver's seat was spookily empty. A car without a driver — the modern incarnation of the headless horseman — was exciting and scary. Exactly like self-managing teams.

"Scrum doesn't care about management. Ideally, there should be no traditional management at all," the trainer kept saying, to the delight of his young audience. Their eyes were glazing with a dreamy haze. It was painful to look at Manoj, who sat at the other end of the room with a stoic expression on his patrician face.

What had we, the managers, done to anger the agilists so much?

If managers, be they sweeter than honey, make decisions, then teams won't take responsibility. "If you're the boss, I'd rather be a dummy," engineers think, as they switch their brains to hibernation mode. The stronger the manager, the weaker the team.

And who cares about a customer somewhere far away in a distant galaxy, when juicy carrots are right here in a manager's hand. Want a bonus? Forget about "customer value." Think how to better please your boss.

One more thing. My ex-boss Yossi told us so many times that we had to deliver "first time right." Which means, never fail. But our trainer kept saying, "a team must learn from its mistakes." It resonated with me — when all is well, my mind sinks into a sweet lazy slumber. I am no Sleeping Beauty — gentle kisses don't wake me up. It's the pain of failure that switches my brain back into action.

Alas, traditional managers don't let their teams fail because managers are held accountable. By not letting teams fail, managers do not let them wake up and learn.

Leviathanian Language

"Vladi, the coach was talking about old-school managers. Don't you remember, we are leaders, not managers here at Leviathan!" said Padma teasingly at the next meeting of our Coconut team.

She was right. Leviathan's language had changed our world.

We, a bunch of MCR barbarians from London, Paris, Jerusalem, and Bangalore, were learning the well-rounded, sugar-coated, politically correct, gender-neutral, non-offensive, heavily sanitized lingo of our new mothership.

We didn't "fire" people anymore. We didn't "sack" them. We didn't "let them go" — even this euphemism sounded too harsh to a delicate corporate ear. Instead, we did a "limited restructuring" or "right-sizing."

No longer did we "hire" or "recruit" people — we "attracted talent." And when this "talent" came onboard, they turned into equally abstract "resources." Beings of flesh and blood were too gross for our neo-spiritual environment.

I thought that race, skin colour, religion, or gender should not be of any concern. What mattered was how clearly, sharply, and freely people think. I was wrong. At Leviathan, the leadership had to ensure not only a diversity of skin colour and gender, but also an "alignment" of the way people think. The word "alignment" was used as often at Leviathan as "achcha" and "pakka" in India.

"I hear you" was a polite way of saying, "I hear you, but will ignore everything you say."

"Thank you for your feedback" meant something like, "Get lost, man."

"Org structure" was not delicate enough, so we said, "taxonomy."

Leviathan did to language what virtuous Mughal conquerors had done to erotic sculptures and carvings in ancient Hindu temples. It cut off everything "indecent" in the language, sterilizing and neutering it. Including Ron's jokes.

I am all for positivity, equality, and inclusivity; I really hate offending people or making anyone feel uncomfortable. Besides, I am under the heavy surveillance of devoted Buddhists, fiery feminists, and animal rights vegan activists in my family. So, to survive, I have to adapt.

I just fail to see how sterilizing our language helps all these noble causes. The way we speak affects the way we think. By wrapping up the language in translucent plastic, we risk choking our creativity. Accepting rules of "compliance" and "alignment," we end up as a herd of conformists.

The word "manager" itself sounded indecent and unsavoury in Leviathanian. After all, the age of managers' uncivilized authoritarian practices had already passed. That's why "managers" were called "leaders" in Leviathanian. As we cautiously say "He-Who-Must-Not-Be-Named" instead of Lord Voldemort.

Leaders did not rely on outdated command-and-control and vulgar authority to get the job done. Instead, sophisticated "leaders" influenced, convinced, and fired up the engineers, inspiring them to ever-greater achievements.

All our "managers" miraculously turned into "leaders" as werewolves at sunrise turn into humans.

But didn't Shakespeare once say, "a manager by any other name would smell as sweet"? If a "leader" has formal subordinates, a bag of carrots, and a formidable stick — this leader is a manager, like it or not. Such a leader has to learn to use those tools efficiently, instead of pretending that they don't exist.

By calling managers "leaders," we implied that personal charisma was all that mattered. No need to care about the hairy issues of organizational structure, roles, responsibilities, and the like.

But it was precisely those issues that were obstructing the flow.

Leaders in Traffic

One day I was stuck in a ridiculous traffic jam — again. Cars, bikes, and scooters had all locked horns, blocking each other to a standstill on the narrow muddy road leading to my house. The traffic policeman had disappeared, so the drivers just kept waiting for him. No one wanted to give way — or even could.

And then, from the very depths of the traffic jam, a natural "leader" emerged — a young man in a stained shirt and cheap rubber sandals. When he got off his scooter to accept the sweet burden of leadership, the god of traffic police apparently entered him. His eyes, like the eyes of that Agni Theyyam performer, started glowing with an unearthly light. I could see his aura palpitating. The young man entered a sort of managerial trance and began giving orders, gesticulating, and screaming at the drivers even more effectively than a real policeman. The drivers obeyed, instantly recognizing in the inspired, if dishevelled, man the Lord of Traffic himself.

Of late, such leaders appear in the thick of Indian traffic more and more often. I am immensely grateful to them — their leadership saves me from the long wait for traffic officers.

The same happens in my office. Teams usually rely on official ("traffic") managers. But in a time of crisis, informal leaders emerge from the depths of corporate swamps and save the day. Their heroism is glorified by corporate communications and rewarded with bonuses.

But what was the root cause of the traffic jams? Not the scarcity of traffic police, for sure — there were thousands of them in Bangalore alone. It was the lack of discipline — drivers simply didn't follow the traffic rules on poorly maintained roads.

Spontaneous "leaders" resolved local issues without addressing their root causes. Thanks to them, the wasteful system didn't have to change. Even worse, when leaders swept the "crowd" after them, the people in the crowd switched their brains into an energy-saving mode. "If she's the leader, she's the one who should think for all."

By glorifying corporate heroes, we trained the system to depend on them. Alex had long advised me to find the most valuable and indispensable engineers — and fire them. Only then would the system figure out how to improve by itself.

Management efforts had to be kept to a minimum. To that end, we would repair the roads and introduce traffic rules. Each of us, from tester to VP, would follow them. Then both the official managers and replacement leaders-heroes would become redundant.

Ladies and gentlemen, why don't we build an organization without leaders?

Vladi the Dracula and Engineering Managers

Very cool. But how exactly?

My drawing of the new Evo sailing ship was still too sketchy, and time was running out. General approaches were clear, but swarms of devils were still playing hide-and-seek in the details.

I was struggling with my Zen koan: "What is the sound of one hand clapping?" How to plug teams without leaders into the Leviathan governance structure? Who will these teams report to?

I kept interrogating experts and gurus, without much success. "Why bother with the org structure at all?" They were surprised by my questions. "Introduce the right Agile mindset. Good engineers can work under any structure!"

Very true. But do they work well because of the org structure (often crooked, ugly, and clumsy) — or despite it? Why do we pay more attention to the architecture of our systems than to the architecture of the organizations that create them in their own organizational image?

I had already seen how our first reorg created the flow of work into India. Please don't "mindset" me — structural changes impact minds better than preaching.

As the saying goes, when the disciple is ready, the guru appears.

We were invited to Atlanta, USA, to spend a week at a hands-on training in a business unit run by Nick, an experienced Leviathan agilist.

It started off on the wrong foot. We arrived inspired, with the glowing eyes of neophytes and a long parchment of questions about scaling up. Instead, our hosts wanted to give us — proud certified Scrum Masters! — an introduction to Agile. They didn't like us to run before we could walk. We didn't like being taught what we already knew.

When Shalini bumped into Nick in the hallway the next morning, tall, lean, and charismatic Nick looked like an ancient prophet of wrath. He was fuming with righteous indignation, furious with the entire Coconut team, and especially with me. To reveal my true evil nature to Shalini, Nick even bothered to Google images of my previous incarnations. "F***ing Vlad the Dracula" and "f***ing Ivan the Terrible," he said in his own peculiar Leviathanian dialect.

Clever Shalini was not too surprised, as she had long since uncovered the dark secrets of my past lives. Under the sunny rays of her tender motherly smile, the storm subsided, and the ice melted. Later I apologized to Nick and his team for the misunderstanding. Nick even agreed to become my personal coach.

Nick had a solution for my Zen koan — not a beautiful one, but pragmatic. He suggested introducing the role of an engineering manager. Each one would care for a few teams so that fewer managers would be required.

Engineering managers don't commit on the delivery dates or scope. They are not Manoj's favourite "one throat to choke" if something goes wrong. What do they do then? They too play curling: engineering managers are technical coaches, not bosses. First, they make sure teams are getting better, with the right education on the best engineering practices.

If our teams are like self-driving cars, Product Owners define their directions, like Google Maps. Scrum

Masters maintain the roads in good shape, fixing pot holes and clearing debris. They also make sure their teams follow the Scrum traffic rules.

Engineering managers take care of the car itself so that the engines, the tires, and the "brains" of the self-driving system work smoothly and reliably. They don't "lead." They don't "encourage." They just service the car.

They also fill the gas tank by distributing salaries and bonuses. Yet, they don't celebrate personal heroism — they capture 360° feedback and reward individual contributions to the team's success.

We would not have believed that such wonderful, fairy-tale unicorns existed in the corporate woods had we not met Nick's right hand — his chief engineering manager. He went out of his way to educate and entertain us, a living embodiment of servant leadership. More caring than a sweet auntie, he brought us tea during the day, and red wine, Scotch, and coke at night. Had we let him, he would have tucked us in when we went to bed.

Still, Nick warned me that we should build checks and balances around engineering managers. Otherwise, from coaches and servants, they would turn into managers and leaders.

Tigers, even tame ones, should be kept in a cage.

Dividing the World

On the way to the airport, we shared our impressions of the few days spent with Nick's team. After a little gossip, we moved on to my favourite topic: what should our structure look like?

"Let's say teams report to engineering managers. And those, who do they report to?"

"God knows..."

"And who do Scrum Masters and Product Owners report to? Engineering managers?"

"In my opinion," Shalini shook her head in disagreement, "it's better for them to be independent. Nick said that the Product Owner is the 'voice of the customer,' and the Scrum Master is the Agile guru and good cop. It is better to keep these roles under separate structures."

Yes, it was better to keep them away from delivery so that they did not succumb to pressures and cut corners. Let them only obey the rules of Scrum. And me, of course, as the perfect embodiment of these rules, heh-heh.

An idea, a truly brilliant one, suddenly illuminated my mind.

"Manoj-ji, why don't you become a chief Scrum Master so that all Scrum Masters and Mistresses work under your wise guidance? The glow of your prestige will shine on the new role. Scrum Masters will be respected if you are their boss!"

Manoj had not yet truly shined as a Scrum Master. Even for his certification exams, he managed to get lower marks than me (and then claimed he did it on purpose to cheer me up). But working as a chief Scrum Master, Manoj would be able to appreciate the beauty of Scrum! It was a high-risk, high-reward move: Scrum Masters under his wise guidance could evolve into project managers. Still worth trying.

But my Machiavellian plan didn't work out. Manoj didn't fancy this role of pure service; he had a much better idea.

"Shalini is going to be a terrific chief Scrum Master, Vladi, much better than me," he admitted, humbly lowering his head. "And Padma is going to be a great chief Product Owner. I can take care of everything else," he modestly nodded in confirmation.

It took me a while to realize that the humble "everything else" meant all engineering managers and their subordinates — about eighty percent of our organization. Well, even now, Manoj was responsible for the biggest team. He was the senior director, while the ladies were just plain vanilla directors.

Padma nervously unlocked and fastened the bracelet of her watch. This was the third, if not the fourth, watch purchased by Padma this year.

Silence.

Shalini said, "No, Manoj. Let's better divide Evo into three regions: Asia, the Americas, and the rest of the world. Each of the three of us will take up business in one of the regions. Engineers working for the regions will report to us. As for the chief Scrum Master and the chief Product Owner, we will find new blood. They will report to Vladi."

It made sense. Each region would develop features important to its customers, on its own; all three organizations would be aligned and co-directed with the flow.

"We still have to reuse features between the regions," said Manoj hesitantly.

Sure thing. But, as my namesake, Lenin, said, "To unite, we must first define lines of demarcation." The more independent my directors were, the easier it was for them to work together. I wouldn't have to persuade them — cooperation would be beneficial for all three of them.

Manoj kept silence, diplomatically — it's not nice to argue about your role in front of your boss. But on the flight, where we sat next to each other, our talk continued.

Angels and Toddlers

This time we were not in my business class habitat, but in economy, tightly pressed together.

The plane had already reached altitude, and the passengers climbed the lower steps of Maslow's pyramid of needs. They were steep, these steps, made up of bread, butter, and chicken pasta instead of business-class delicacies. Now it was time to have some wine and climb higher up Maslow's pyramid — to the need of communication.

"I truly respect Shalini," Manoj leaned confidentially toward me, "but how can you entrust a third of our business to a person who has never done delivery?"

After a couple of glasses of red wine, I easily agreed — sure, Manoj, you take Asian customers. Padma can take Europe and Africa, and Shalini can take the Americas, where we have very few customers. Manoj's share was larger than that of Shalini and Padma combined. Still, his monopoly on delivery would be broken.

A nice, smiling Indian family with a baby occupied the row behind us. The little cutie pie kicked my seat with such joyous persistence that it seemed she had found her true purpose in life. Now I knew what trees think of woodpeckers. There was no way I could sleep, so I pulled out my laptop.

Checking emails was like clearing of snow during a snowfall. No matter how much you clear, new snow piles up. I got hundreds of emails daily. Wi-Fi on Lufthansa flights was usually patchy, but this time the communication beam from the satellite to the plane was impeded neither by random UFOs, nor by flocks of stray angels. Seventy-six new emails in the inbox were craving my attention:

The issues of Malaysian project integration... they were a ticking time bomb.

Evo's successful launch in Latin America, albeit with a delay of two and a half months. Still, well done to the team.

A couple of dozen emails from Leviathan on the topic of the never-ending integration.

And what was this?... Oh, no! Our anonymous author strikes again!

Anonymous Email

This email was sent from a whistle-blowing address: "concerned-leviathan-employee@gmail.com." The entire management team, including Sandra, was on the recipient list. Among the numerous fascinating points brought up in this lengthy email, there was a mention of Krishna.

Favouritism is one of the many issues in a dysfunctional organization headed by Vladi. Just to give an example. It was only through subservience and ingratiation with Vladi that Krishna K. managed to get the role of an account manager in Mumbai, which he is completely incompetent to fulfil.

As our ex-CEO used to say, "et cetera."

This was not our first anonymous letter. The first one, a few years ago, accused the director of our French line of frequently sending his lieutenant to relax in Paris and paying him hefty bonuses in exchange for kickbacks. Both were allegedly engaged in real estate business during working hours. In addition, both "mentally harassed" their subordinates by not recognizing their achievements and not helping their career growth.

All those mentioned were questioned by a special MCR Inquisition Committee. Lie detectors, waterboarding, fire torture, and mass spectrometry confirmed that the head of the French line was in the clear. After receiving a few more anonymous emails — beautiful fruits of pure creative imagination — the MCR management got used to them. But Sandra was not familiar with our epistolary traditions. She would get to the bottom of it.

Anyway, the style of this email was different from the previous ones. And why, of all my sins, was I accused of the one I was not guilty of?

Krishna was one of our project managers. Recently, an account manager position opened in the sales department in Mumbai. Krishna applied, and I supported his transition; a friend would be even more useful to us on the other side of the barricade — in the sales department. The decision to take Krishna on board had been made by sales' senior managers, but for some reason, I was to blame for it.

It hurt. While I was trying to save our ship, one of my crew, using an anonymous email address as a Harry Potter invisibility cloak, tried to throw me overboard.

SAFe and Indra-net

The next morning, heavily jetlagged, we went for SAFe (Scaled Agile Framework) training — to expand our horizons and see what SAFe practices we could use. It turned out we could use everything; all our outdated structures could easily fit on the soft and cosy Procrustean bed of SAFe. We could scale up the operating model of Scrum to the level of the entire organization without changing much, just renaming the roles.

Our well-rounded, smiling lecturer said, "The changes must be done in an evolutionary manner, step by step. We should also be pragmatic about integration. Integration is inevitable in large software organizations; we just need to do it optimally." Indeed, the "Release Train Engineer" (RTE) sounds much more "optimal" than "the integrator."

The longer we listened to the talkative lecturer, the more it seemed that he was ready to put the seal of kashrut or halal on any unholy pig, just to please the customer. Still, he admitted, you had to start by laying down the foundation of Scrum.

The gospel offers a parable. One man built a house on a rock, and his house withstood all calamities. Another one built his on sand. This house could not withstand the rain and the wind — "and great was its fall." In my corporate world, there are no "great falls" — it's always a success. It's just that some proclaimed successes end up in projects terminations and "limited restructuring."

My coach from the States, Nick, also warned us about SAFe built on a weak, shabby Scrum. On his advice, we'd start with strong Scrum, and then we'd figure out how to scale it up, if at all. There were already too many smart frameworks on the market — SAFe, LeSS, Scrum, DevOps, Kanban, Spotify, Lean, The Toyota Way, Scrum@Scale....

Begun as a revolt against Big Stupid Organizations and Processes, Agile had been domesticated, tamed, divided into factions, and absorbed by the very corporate world it rebelled against. Many of its founding fathers opened their shops in the Temple of Agile to sell their methodologies and frameworks. They all seemed to be different, but they were so similar. They almost reflected each other, like mirrors facing each other.

"Have you heard of Indra net, Vladi-ji?"

"Intranet? Like, our corporate intranet?"

"No," Manoj laughed politely. "Lord Indra's net — the net of the god Indra! It encompasses the whole world. Each of its nodes is a pure diamond; each diamond reflects all other nodes and its own reflections in them, to infinity. A kind of fractal."

The world of software is like the Indra-net: our texts and ideas are endlessly reflected in each other. Let's see how our node — our interpretation of the Agile and DevOps — turned out. Our innovation was not to invent anything new; we just had to reflect the best around us.

Love, Actually

Our HR director called me up urgently, in the middle of the SAFe course. Krishna had just told her that yesterday someone called his wife to inform her that Krishna had a secret girlfriend in Mumbai, and this affair was the real reason for Krishna seeking the transfer. Krishna's wife was in tears. She had no clue who called her.

Uh-oh... Not good at all.

I called up Ramesh, our IT director, to check if by chance yesterday's call to Krishna's wife was made from the office.

In the evening, when the training was already over, Ramesh called me back.

"Vladi, my team checked outgoing calls and CCTV footage, actually...."

"And?"

"Well, this was Radha, actually...." Ramesh was almost embarrassed.

"Who is Radha?"

"A QC engineer. She works for Krishna... Actually, she called his wife...." Ramesh sounded so upset and apologetic.

"Did she write that email?"

"We don't know, actually... Do you want me to check?"

No, of course not. Writing anonymous emails to the top brass was the sacred right of every employee, but disturbing families was not.

What I thought was a devilish plot to get me fired was, in reality, a Bollywood love story gone too far. But what a character, this Radha.... How much she loved this guy, to risk her career and her reputation just to keep him by her side. Her passion was beautiful and scary. Abominable and divine at the same time.

We didn't need gods and goddesses — just developers and testers. She had to leave.

They say that many girls fell madly in love with Lord Krishna. It's tough to be a god — Lord Krishna had sixteen thousand wives. A tad too many for most mortals. As for Krishna, he created as many copies of himself as he wanted. So, he bestowed his divine love on all his wives every night.

Our Krishna — broad-faced, big-boned, with large black laughing eyes, riding an expensive motorcycle — was also a ladies' man, like the god after whom he was named. This was not his first turbulent story in the office. He'd better learn to clone himself.

PART III. THE PROPHET MOSES AND THE BURNING LAKE

Executive Leadership — Portrait d'Intérieur

Soon I had to fly to the States again, this time to Leviathan's California headquarters for the annual executive leadership conference. When you — the only vice president in India — find yourself in a huge conference room packed with vice and other presidents, you are put in your place.

After giving an account of the past year's achievements and the next three years' strategy, Leviathan's president looked around the hall with a piercing x-ray glance from under bushy eyebrows and invited the audience to comment.

A whole forest of hands shot up. Each of the vice-presidents wanted to share their deepest feelings. "As a true servant leader, I am 'all in' with the Leviathan's vision; I am absolutely aligned with the strategy, and

I am super-excited to execute it. I am grateful from the bottom of my heart to the members of the operating committee and personally to Mr. President for his great leadership. I promise full cooperation and blah-blah-blah teamwork and blah-blah-blah 'achieving business outcomes' and blah-blah execute and blah-blah align blah-blah-blah…"

I swear I saw tears on the cheeks of servant leaders overwhelmed with enthusiasm. It was like taking a time machine to my happy childhood in Soviet Russia, with its "exciting" and "inspiring" Communist party Plenums.

I usually get sea-sick from time travelling.

When the applause subsided, a guest speaker ran up to the podium — a young technical director of one of Leviathan's largest customers. I couldn't believe my ears when this guy in jeans and a t-shirt said, "I need end-to-end solutions, and you offer me separate, poorly integrated products, each from their own business unit. Your business units compete with each other! Stop sending me moulds of your organization structure. Get yourselves together and think about your customer needs and end-to-end solutions!"

His speech was also met with a round of applause. Well, not as enthusiastic as our president's, but still. That chap paid Leviathan hundreds of millions of dollars a year. For that kind of money, he could say anything. And even the truth would be greeted with clapping hands.

It was interesting how Evo's issues of "component vs. end-to-end" repeated themselves on a completely different, cosmic level. During our honeymoon after the MCR acquisition, we spent a week with Leviathan's top management. The crème-de-la-crème of American management, each responsible for billions of dollars of revenue, with smiles brighter than a dentist's ad, privately complained to us — in the system of checks and balances created by the president, none of them could move ahead. They blocked each other like cars in Bangalore's traffic jams. On the bright side, no one of them could get ahead of the others — and that's what the checks and balances were for.

At the corporate dinner after the conference, I had a chat with a seasoned Leviathanian leader from Sandra's team. I wondered what he thought of the day's self-indulgent sucking up.

My teammate didn't quite get my naïve question. "What are you talking about? Of course, you have to get noticed to move up!"

I had some cultural issues with being "noticed": in Soviet schools, I was taught to keep quiet if I didn't have anything smart to say. And to keep even quieter when I had — it was safer that way.

Since we could not align in joint condemnation of sycophancy, I thought of moving on to a neutral and safe topic. Like India.

"India? Vladi, how can you live in that rotten country,

with all its filth and bureaucracy? Developers don't know how to write code there, and managers are useless. Eastern Europe is much better for outsourcing. So, what do you think, how to fix India?"

Holy cow... I had heard this question before. I hated it.

"You can't 'fix' India, man. India is a reality, a given. Go fix yourself and the way you work with India," I intended to say.

But I didn't utter a word, stunned by cognitive dissonance: firstly, this well-rounded corporate intellectual was an Indian himself, born and raised "in that rotten country" — in Kerala. Had the stars aligned differently, a goddess might have entered him.

And secondly, he had several hundred engineers working for him at Chennai — and he praised them left, right, and centre! How come?

"Of course, my team is good, but they are such a rare exception, Vladi!"

I had heard that in the past, from leaders and managers, "My Indians are better than your Indians because I am their leader."

This consistency in our rapidly changing world was reassuring.

After the conference, I knew exactly what I didn't want. The details still had to be worked out.

Agile Religion

We already knew what our org topology, metrics, and delivery pipelines would look like. Our self-driving teams would work according to strict Scrum rules. That way, our masterpiece — the drawing of the Evo ship on the wall, its operating model — was almost ready.

But how to turn our diagrams and PowerPoint slides into a real sailing boat? And how to bring more than a thousand engineers onboard?

Should we leap into freedom, asking teams to self-organize and experiment? Should we go prescriptive and top-down? Should we start small and scale up later?

Agile consultants and gurus mostly agreed, "Teams should be free to choose whichever framework they want. Management and org structure don't matter; it's all about servant leadership and Agile mindset. Big bang approach never works — you can't boil the ocean. Start small, then scale up."

But each conversation ended with the same disclaimer: "Think for yourself — each case is unique."

Flipping through endless transformation articles, on the verge of silent desperation, I stumbled upon a curious debate: is Agile a religion of sorts? Agile opponents insisted, "Sure, Agile is a religion, with its 'rituals,' Scrum master priests and fanatical adepts." Agile backers fiercely fought back, "No, Agile is no creed!"

To cleanse Agile from the slightest taint of a religious approach and adjust it to new corporate realities, Scrum's "backlog grooming" was discreetly renamed "refinement." And dubious "rituals" became neutral "events." That way, Scrum slowly turned into yet another soulless "process" — good for corporate artificial intelligence, not necessarily for the humans of emotional India.

While arguing, both sides shared the same assumption: religions are dogmatic and non-questioning. No one questioned this very assumption, which was utterly wrong. Religions are built around doubt and debate!

Discussions between Arjuna and Krishna form the core of the Bhagavad-Gita. The thick volumes of the Jewish Talmud are nothing but the records of fierce disputes in the high schools of Babylon and Jerusalem. Rules, laws, and God himself were ferociously questioned there. I've seen the philosophical debates in Buddhist monasteries (and couldn't understand a word as I don't know Tibetan or Pali; even my Leviathanian is far from fluent).

Critical thinking is important for both modern and traditional cultures. Still, there is a difference.

Modern culture shoots from the hip: this doesn't work for us, we should change it. This is exactly how my mind works: I want to redo everything, immediately, and make it much better. Only when I start reinventing the wheel do I realize why it is round.

For Western programmers, philosophy, religion, and spirituality are "spherical cows in a vacuum" — abstract, detached-from-reality dogmatic bullcrap. As my tough and ferocious Eastern European colleague used to say, "What can't be written in Java can't be true." I wonder how he can express this deep philosophical thought in Java code.

India is different. Here, almost everyone is religious, at least to some extent. Ravi, the manager of our French line, got up at three in the morning to study the Vedas. Manoj was very serious about yoga and the teachings of Osho. Even Padma — not the most ardent devotee of Hinduism — taught her sons tradition so that they could choose what, how, and if to follow when they grow up.

Age-old traditions know something about transformation and adaptability that endless articles and hordes of OCM (organizational change management) gurus don't.

To my embarrassment, I didn't know much about Hinduism, Jainism, or Islam, shame on me.

But I knew a thing or two about management and Judaism.

Marx and Moses

At the weekly meeting of the Coconut team, I shared my theological insights on organizational transformation:

Please sit back... No, no, no preparations for sleep, Manoj! Intravenous coffee, please — and get ready for enlightenment!

One of the first case studies of a large-scale transformation is described in the biblical drama of Exodus. When God brought the Jews out of slavery in Egypt, they were not a "people" yet but a motley, unruly, "unaligned" crowd. "Erev rav" — a mixed multitude, as the Bible calls them.

What did Moses do as their "transformation leader"?

No, he didn't deliver inspirational sermons about the beauty of moral values and the importance of unity, like our president. Tradition says that Moses was tongue-tied, not great at public speaking. In Leviathan, he wouldn't reach even a director's level.

To bring this diverse crowd into one, from the dazzling summit of Mount Sinai, Moses brought his people the Tablets of the Law, not the Tablets of the Spirit. That is, he introduced common practices. What we practice defines what we believe in. What we do determines who we are.

The huge crowd didn't chant back, "We believe you!" or "We believe in God!" Instead, they replied to Moses with some scepticism, "Na'aseh V'nishma" — "Let's do it first. And then we will figure it out." We will understand the Law by practicing it.

The practice of the Law had moulded a disjointed, rebellious crowd into one (if rather stubborn) people. Until now, Judaism does not have a spiritual or ecclesiastical hierarchy or formal dogmas of faith. In Hinduism, too, there is no chief Hindu Pope or cardinals. People scattered all over the world — both Jews and Hindus — are connected by a way of life, not by beliefs. It's performing Puja (prayer practices) or putting on Tefillin, observing Shabbat and holidays, lighting Jewish Hanukkah or Indian Diwali candles.

A distant descendant of Moses, Karl Marx, said, "Being" (how we live — our place in the social hierarchy — and our personal interests and needs) determines "consciousness" — thoughts, opinions, and beliefs. Thinking is not "pure reasoning" but a quirky advocate of our interests, benefits, and desires.

If we appoint Manoj to lead development, instead of Padma, he will start fighting with the project managers — his current subordinates — in no time. And if Padma takes over project management instead of Manoj, she will decide that poor development practices are the root of all evil.

We encourage people to "work together" and "follow corporate principles," but people don't change because of speeches (even their own). People change when they have to adapt to new realities. We will change realities from the very core — from metrics to structures to frameworks.

"Vladi, I'm sorry, this is all terribly interesting, but your spherical cow has just jumped into a vacuum... Could you please be a little more specific?" Vijay said, smiling.

"I am sorry, Vijay, I can't. I am on a roll. Give me five more minutes, please!"

Scrum and the Tablets of the Covenant

"When Moses gave his people the Tablets of the Covenant with the ten commandments, the people did not say, 'Sure, we will stop killing. But we will continue with adultery, as this practice fits our organizational culture!'

"Or, 'We are ready to observe the Sabbath but honouring our father and mother would be too much! Still we can do a pilot project on 'respect.'

"No, people accepted the ten commandments as a holistic system — as a set menu rather than à la carte.

"Let's assume that Scrum is a complete, well-thought-out system where all the elements are interconnected. Then we have to implement Scrum rigorously — as close to the Scrum guide as possible. We can't introduce the role of a Product Owner and also keep Project Managers. We can't establish the role of a Scrum Master but make them responsible for deliveries. And so on. Let's assume that Scrum is a single precise mechanism with many gears working together, like a clock."

"What if it isn't?" asked Padma.

"Then we're in the soup. But if we assume the opposite — that Scrum is a set of ingredients, and each team must come up with their own recipe — we simply don't have enough time. We will need six years, not six months.

"It's like Pascal's famous wager, 'If a religion is false, you risk a small loss by believing it to be true. If religion is true, you risk everything (like an eternity in Hell) by believing it to be false.' We take a leap of faith — accept the adaptive model as a whole, trusting that it can save us. Good engineers can make any model work — if they trust it."

I paused. The room was quiet — no enthusiastic clapping. My teammates' faces weren't too sour, but they didn't look happy either. I got it — I'd just proposed a strict top-down implementation of the operating model. Although packaged in all sorts of metaphors, it made me feel uneasy, too. In a different culture, in a different situation, I would ask the teams to define their own ways of work.

But I was where I was.

"Why did you let the guys define our old *process* by themselves?" asked Padma. "It worked great back then!"

Before I was ready to reply, I got unexpected support from Shalini.

"That time we didn't shift the paradigm. The teams just articulated what they already knew. Now we're in uncharted territory. I agree with Vladi — teams need clarity first. Freedom will come later when teams learn the new model in practice. Without hands-on experience, teams can't define their way of work!"

Thank you, Shalini! I listened to Padma and Murali when it came to architecture and technology. But when it came to relationships and processes, Shalini was my compass.

In a traditional culture, workers start with a humble apprenticeship — sweeping floors or mixing paints. Then they become journeymen and work for themselves, but within the established rules, defined by

the masters. After many years of practice, some journeymen evolve into masters. The masters are not
limited by tradition — they ARE the tradition.

Funny... I was not religious or traditional at all, and I
didn't like following rules. How could I get so carried
away?

How to Boil the Ocean

It was already late. Shalini's husband couldn't pick
her up — Misha, their daughter, was not feeling well.
The family had chosen a cute Russian name for the little girl — "Misha." Too bad that in Russia it's a boy's
name.

I gave a ride to Shalini and to Padma, too — she left her
scooter at the office and would pick it up tomorrow.

We continue our conversation in the car — that's why
I offered them a ride.

"What do you ladies think, should we change the entire organization in one go, or start with a small trial
first?"

"If we do a pilot, our guys will say, 'Well, they have
selected an easy project' and 'Management was too
helpful.' Those who do not want to be convinced will
not be convinced either way," said Shalini.

"Yeah!" Padma agreed for a change. "We all know
that Scrum works in small teams; there is nothing to

prove. What we need to prove is scaling up. And we can't prove scaling up on a small pilot. So why waste time?"

They say, "You can't boil the ocean." But that's exactly what we needed — to boil our ocean. It would take years to boil it kettle by kettle.

We dropped Padma off and drove on.

I'd been keen to talk to Shalini for a long time. Both the fiery impulsiveness of Padma and the calmness of traditional Manoj resonated with me. They could both be wrong, just like me. But Shalini was the biggest mystery in the office. She was like a different species.

In the West, we often get stuck in internal dramas: we know what we should do, but we end up doing the opposite. We are torn between "spirit" and "flesh," between "must" and "want." We can't do even what we want without procrastination. But Shalini... she knew what is right instinctively as if prompted by her DNA — and always did the right thing.

"I don't get what you mean, Vladi. What 'internal conflicts'? I do what I have to do, and that's what I want to do. Why would I do the wrong thing?"

Had Shalini not cried a couple of times in my office, I would have taken her for an artificial intelligence.

"You know, there are very few people like you in our world, Shalini!"

"No, my whole family is like this. We are about eighty people, very tightly knit."

"Hmm… can't be that none of you have ever done anything wrong!"

I deliberately provoked; Shalini pondered for a while.

"You know, when I was in third grade, I lived with my aunt. Once I took a pen from a classmate, without her permission. And brought it home. In our family, everyone is treated the same, children, nephews, and nieces. My auntie scolded me as much as her own daughter. I was terribly ashamed, and I have never done anything like that again!"

Oh my God! Did I have a Buddha on my payroll?

"I get it. Stealing a fountain pen in third grade is a grave sin indeed — the worst your family has committed in generations. Well, what about family life? Nothing spicy? No adultery? No divorces?"

"Not really. Wait, there was one exceptional case; my great-grandfather had two women! But he didn't hide it from anyone. He talked to his first wife, and she agreed because she was very happy with him; he did everything for her. Only then did he take another woman, and he built her a separate house. Maybe it's not so moral, but there was no cheating, you know? Times are changing now; so are we. What was not allowed before is permitted now."

"Like what?"

"Previously, all marriages were arranged by parents. Now we can even... how to say... have an affair. But only once in a lifetime, and it must end in marriage."

Shalini talked from experience — she was married to one of our engineers. The trajectory of her career was much steeper than his, and this was an issue in such a traditional country.

We were already approaching Shalini's house.

"I'm just curious, Shalini, do you ever read Western books? Like, fiction?"

"Not really, Vladi. But sometimes I watch Hollywood movies — to understand how other people live and how my family and I should deal with such people."

I was, of course, one of "such people." As for Shalini, she looked more like Homo Sapiens than any other alien I had ever met. And I had met a few.

After dropping off Shalini, Rajesh the driver took me home along Bellandur Lake. This lake is one of the unsung wonders of the world (and an ecological catastrophe): it emits massive amounts of cheerful and eerie cloudy foam. Overflowing and getting out of the lake in dirty flakes, this foam — most likely sentient — crawls along the nearby streets, seeping into houses and cars. Local newspapers often mention the mischievous adventures of the Bellandurian foam.

There are more wonders to this lake. From time to time, its water bursts into flames and burns for long hours. Monstrous industrial pollution is the cause. But it was still inspiring to me — if the lake could catch fire, then the ocean could be boiled!

Thanks to this startlingly blazing lake, which I was driving alongside, I had finally made up my mind. Against all common-sense recommendations, our transformation was going to be driven from the top, with rigid discipline and consistency across the whole organization.

I was betting on command-and-control to move away from command-and-control for good.

Evo was like a hedgehog in the Russian saying: a proud bird — unless you kick it upwards, it won't fly.

Meta-management in the Himalayas

I was always so busy at work that I could hardly ever take a leave. But this time the stars aligned, and I flew to Dharamshala and Ladakh in the Indian Himalayas for a short but intense trip with my friends. At first, I dearly regretted it. Towards the end of our four-day trek across the Chang La pass ("baby track," as our guides called it), I could hardly crawl.

But then I didn't want to go back to Bangalore. Ancient Buddhist monasteries were so naturally blended into the lunar, rocky landscape that the mountains seemed to grow out of them, blooming with huge snowy flowers. The silence had been so solemn that I could hear it even later, looking at the pictures I had taken there. I finally found where to be born next time. And to spend a few lifetimes, dissolving in the profound serenity of the Himalayas.

In my current incarnation, I found myself insoluble. During focused Buddhist meditations, my white monkey mind either fell asleep or kept fussing around, thinking about work. Hatred as tender as froth on boiled milk was quietly forming inside my mind, right on top of the prescribed love for all sentient beings.

The nano-enlightenment that I experienced was also related to work. In my meditative half-sleep, I suddenly realized that the desire to be a leader — even the "service leader" that Agile keeps praising — is an ego game. From the height of the Himalayas, it looked petty. Service is beautiful in itself, but not as a means to get ahead of other people and "lead" them. Why bother?

I was thinking again of the meta-management and quiet non-action of the Tao, which I had almost forgotten about. Meta-action instead of fussing around. Creating conditions for the flow, instead of pushing against it.

We went to see the sources of the sacred Ganges. I obviously needed this vacation. Even looking at a rocky area with numerous waterfalls, streams, and rivers, all I saw was an unfolding metaphor for my organization.

An organization is a land of small creeks and bigger rivulets flowing into one mighty river — the main value stream. It is running from an idea in someone's wise mind to a solution deployed for a delighted customer.

Often the organization's landscape — its structures and processes — impede the flow. Then, the Sisyphean labour of "leaders" is required to make its waters flow upward. Leaders coordinate, remind, lead, and kick the engineers' stubborn behinds. Poor things, leaders work so hard.

Still, they should not be pitied. Hard work provides them with meaning and purpose, and justifies their existence: "Oh, we are so busy! Nothing moves without us! We are so valuable and irreplaceable!" To make themselves "important," managers create a mess in their organizations without even realizing it.

If managers have to "work hard" and preach to everyone about "teamwork," these are the symptoms of a sick organization in need of change. It means the landscape of structures and processes has to be terraformed. Personal and group interests have to align with the flow of value.

For terraforming (or simply, reorg), meta-managers use the heavy machinery of command-and-control. But when the terraforming is complete, their job is immensely enjoyable: to look after the flow of value through the ecosystem and remove obstacles in its path. To carry away a fallen (code) trunk blocking a rivulet. Cleaning up a small data lake full of algae. Also, subduing and taming someone's ego — most often, the manager's very own.

Meta-managers work "less" — not timewise, but substance-wise. Delivery happens as if by itself, calmly and smoothly, almost effortlessly, without heroic acts or firefighting. And without leaders, too.

Meta-managers are almost invisible. Their presence is unnoticed, but their absence is strongly felt.

When I returned to Bangalore, I regretfully admitted that I was not a very good Buddhist. I could not achieve happiness by changing my psyche and my reactions to external events. But maybe there was still a chance for me to become a good manager. If you can't become the Count of Monte Cristo, you should try to be happy as a janitor.

I was ready to boil the ocean.

PART IV. OCEAN ON FIRE

Desert, Palace, and Freedom

One email to the entire Evo division was enough to set our ocean (some would say "our swamp") on fire.

The email announced the transition to a new model. We took apart the entire integration department, the entire testing department, and all component development teams — and formed cross-functional feature teams instead. Formally, these teams reported to engineering managers. In reality, they were only subordinate to the rules of the operating model and the customers. Engineering managers under three regional directors took care of the teams' "technical excellence," training, and such trifles as salaries and bonuses. Only the teams, not the managers, were responsible for the deliveries.

Rest in peace, project management office. You served us well, but your earthly journey has come to an end.

All Scrum Masters reported to the chief Scrum Master, and all Product Owners reported to the chief Product Owner. Both chiefs reported to me, not to the directors, to keep the Scrum people as far away from delivery as possible.

How do you prevent self-driving teams from driving too far away from each other? How do you make all engineers share their pain, experience, code, and knowledge? We laced people across different teams into "guilds" — engineering communities without formal subordination. The software industry is still young and wet behind its ears. So it is searching for its roots in the Middle Ages, when communities of free masters followed traditions of craftsmanship, and quality was a virtue.

Code moderators — senior developers and integrators — also formed a guild. Moderators were our code trunk custodians. Like all other developers, they wrote code. But they spent a couple of hours of post-lunch siesta reviewing other people's masterpieces.

We could not convert all the teams to the new structure in one go, as we had to train them. So we divided the thousand-plus people into four giant ocean "waves," one after the other, and published a calendar of training and transitioning into the new model. Same training for all ensured a common language and a common frame of reference.

The playbook summarized it, defining who does what, how, when, and why. Engineers had been promised freedom, but they had got more rules and restrictions than before. We already knew it; freedom needs a framework. People should follow it, but after six months, once they gain experience, they can rise up against it. Without the rules, there are no rebellions.

The playbook allowed only Scrum meetings — "events." All other meetings were banned to save precious development time. A special procedure was required for an exception.

This was tough for Manoj. In the past, he used to summon the council of elders in his office, listening to everyone and making the right decision. Now calling everyone who mattered was not allowed. Besides, it was no longer clear who mattered.

It was high time for our wall painting of a new Evo boat to come to life. As our chief Kabbalah officer, Shalini volunteered to make it happen. She was working on the nitty-gritty of training, coordination, and other mundane aspects of the miracle, in addition to ruling her part of the business world — Americas.

In the past, we had been putting out fires in one project or another. This time we were in the middle of a flaming ocean, on a half-burnt sailing boat, caught in the blaze of our corporate Agni Theyyam.

Who would pull us out of the fire if we got too carried away?

Coaches with Zen Rulers

Nick advised me to hire transformational coaches. First, they would make sure that police — "managers" and "leaders" — did not self-originate in the corporate primordial soup. Second, they would give the Coconut team continuous feedback. And third, they would train teams in the mechanics of our operating model. And set up the Scrum scaffolding.

In one of the deep pockets on the warm Leviathan belly, we found the money for coaches. Now we had to find the coaches.

Agile coaches were plenty. Most of them were experts in the mechanics of Scrum but not of much help with delivery pipelines, org structure, engineering practices, and everything else required for frequent releases. The moment a new candidate started explaining to me that "Agile is a mindset," "org structure doesn't really matter," or "no, I don't have DevOps experience, but as a servant leader, I..." — the interview was over.

Besides, most Indian coaches were too soft and fluffy, too malleable. Too ready to adapt to our realities instead of changing them.

But the stars aligned, and through the mysterious trails of Agile networking, Jack — an experienced coach from the States — found us. He looked like a kind grandfather with an unruly silver beard, silver hair, and shimmering affectionate eyes. His looks concealed his true nature. By trade and creed Jack was the Ripper of Managers.

Always comfortably dressed in Indian kurtas, with a permanently glued detached smile — a trademark of Buddhist monks and Agile coaches — Jack trained teams to think for themselves. If someone tried to lead and dominate, Jack would whiplash the wall with his meter ruler, slapping the poor wall so brutally and suddenly that everyone startled. Zen masters use the sudden slap of a stick to bring their students to enlightenment. The slamming of Jack's Zen ruler made the teams aware that strong personalities do not matter. Teams work for customers!

Actually, not even "for" customers but with them. Without customers on board, our boat was not going to fly. To persuade them to switch to the new model, I went on a tour of "exotic countries" without any monkeys, elephants, or auto rickshaws. I visited our customers in their habitat.

A stern, unsmiling technical director in Sweden asked me when it was better to switch — now or after the big release in six months.

"Depends on when you want to hear bad news about this release — in two weeks or in six months," I explained, not so much to him as to myself.

My knees were trembling.

Anyway, all our customers had agreed to allocate people and start working with us under the new rules. They hadn't much to lose. For each customer, we started with a two-day workshop with Jack and his coaches in Bangalore. Our engineers, our partners from other Leviathan development centres, and the customers' representatives were trained together as one team.

Customers and our Product Owners learned techniques for prioritizing and slicing features as thinly as carpaccio so that something of value for end-users could be released in two weeks. In the evenings, the teams played bowling and... umm... jointly consumed alcoholic beverages. I had never invested the company's money better than in this alcohol-based lubrication of our ecosystem's gears.

Steam Engine, Kettle, and Quality

In the corporate world, work is always in progress, and progress is always fast. But how much of the work is completed remains in question. What "completed" means is another question.

Therefore, the playbook has clearly defined what "done" means: the code is ready only when it is tested across all customer projects. The test automation is written. And there are no bugs.

Our developers gently enquired which planet of the solar system we had come from. No bugs? Rubbish! Bugs are a given; how can we do without them?

We said, "Bugs are evil, and the older they are, the more evil they are." The developers who introduce bugs eventually get distracted, move to another project, quit, or die of old age. Therefore, fixing bugs becomes much more expensive over time. Like in the old joke about the steam engine and a kettle, bugs should be killed while they are young.

"What joke, Vladi?" asked Manoj.

He knew it. He also knew I liked telling it. It was from my dubious treasury of vintage corporate jokes. An old man suddenly stands up and shatters a whistling tea kettle with a hammer. But why? In his youth, he was almost run over by a steam locomotive. To prevent kettles from growing into steam engines, he kills them young.

The easiest way to fix a bug is to prevent it. If you can't write a thousand lines of code without bugs — write a hundred. Even a hundred is too much? Write ten. You think it's too slow? Still, it's always faster and cheaper than fixing bugs later! And if a bug has crept in, it should be caught immediately, before it grows into a steam engine. The time between the developers submitting the code and getting back the results of testing should be minutes, not weeks.

However, our sad delivery pipeline was chronically

constipated. The code could barely squeeze through the quality gates. Manual testing took weeks. Test automation was patchy, unreliable, and so unstable that developers never knew if the bug was in their code or if it was another bug in the automation system itself. So teams thought that test automation was a kind of corporate bureaucracy preventing them from moving faster.

Vijay started the overhaul of our delivery pipeline. We usually did everything ourselves, but this time we hired contractors to get the results sooner and to start killing bugs younger.

What Is in It for Me?

Top leadership usually gets transformation right. Why shouldn't they? They keep their jobs, and their work becomes even more interesting and meaningful. They believe that they are part of the solution, not the problem.

The real problem is with the middle management — component owners, project and program managers, QA managers — you name it. They have done no evil, working the way they were asked to, for many years. Good, honest, hard-working people, the backbone of our organization.

In other words, the bastion of command-and-control and the first target of a headcount reduction.

We announced, "There will be no component, project, or program management anymore. One can become a Scrum Master, a Product Owner, an engineering manager, or better yet — a developer or a tester. We are looking for seniors to be technical and hands-on!"

To put it gently, these options didn't fill our managers' hearts with joy.

"What is in it for me?" The disoriented middle managers scratched their heads. "What is my career going to be? A senior Scrum Master? And then what? Self-driving teams sound nice, but who has the real power?"

None of the new roles were tempting, since none of them gave the coveted personal responsibility for delivery.

Deprived of their corporate property and stripped of their rights and regalia, the former leaders felt confused and persecuted, like Russian nobility after the Communist revolution.

Some managed to reinvent themselves as Scrum Masters or Product Owners; others had to accept such humble work as writing code. But most of them could not find any place for themselves on our burning ship.

A strong, meticulous program manager — one of our best — was convinced she had to manage information flows tightly. In other words, she decided who should know what about her program, and gave out this information bit by bit. Being a strong manager, she just refused to unblock the communication lines. She had to go — the adaptive model with its collectivism and transparency was not for her.

One of our project managers set up a one-on-one with me:

"Vladi, please ask around! Everyone will tell you that I am a good servant leader. I get the job done without forcing anyone!"

Indeed, he did not use force; instead, he received instructions from his British colleagues and passed them on to the team in India. Then he sent the reports he harvested from his subordinates back to London. After discussing the differences between leadership and the postal service, he had to go.

The hierarchy was falling apart. It was not easy for the more experienced people to compete with their younger teammates — experience in the old model was a hindrance in the new one.

A manager applied for the position of a Scrum master on a big project. It turned out that his former subordinate, Reshmi, applied for the same role. The manager, an honest and straightforward person, told her what he thought, "You don't have the technical skills. You don't have the charisma. You will never be a Scrum Master, take my word for it!"

Poor Reshmi wept for several days. Just a few weeks

later, she became one of our best Scrum Masters, rolling around the office like a nimble ferocious fireball, attacking my directors and me to resolve her team's dependencies.

Her former manager stopped by to say goodbye before leaving.

I smiled back at the tense, shyly smiling people whom I fired; I shook their sweaty hands. Even those who didn't need money had feelings, aspirations, and hopes. Almost everyone thanked me for their good experience with MCR India in the past, and those thanks hurt the most. If this situation was anyone's fault, it was mine, not theirs — I should have transformed Evo much earlier. Still, I was the one wishing them luck in their future careers, not the other way round.

Within a couple of months, we lost more than half of our middle managers.

In Agile, they say, "embrace the change." It turned out that I had to embrace the pain that comes with the change. My karma didn't get better, and neither did my spirits.

Korean Warriors and Indian Yogis

Sandra, our boss, kept communicating with the five

thousand employees of the former MCR and the Leviathan departments that have joined us. In her last video message, she was as optimistic as ever. Although the former MCR faced some challenges, she expressed full confidence in our long-term success. Of course, alignment and stricter product unification would be necessary to achieve it.

Every word of her speech was meticulously measured and brought to perfection by the best corporate communications experts. But you can't be partially authentic, just like you can't be half pregnant. After Sandra's life-affirming speech, the faces in the office turned even more sullen.

Among other decisions, Sandra announced that our Korean office would be "right-sized." Its right size was zero — the office was closing. The Korean engineers were asked to transfer their projects to India. But they left immediately, without even serving their notice period — the job market in Seoul was hot.

I recalled our first meeting with MCR Korea. As in a bad joke, Brits, Israelis, French, Koreans, Indians, and Americans got together in Paris. It was an internal conference led by our now-former boss, Yossi, senior VP Development.

There were no surprises in our usual monotonous corporate show-off until Dong-Ju, the general manager of the newly established Korean site, started his presentation. Wearing a suit as formal as if he were at a funeral, the slim Korean leader was hammering in messages as hard as nails:

"Writing code, integration, and testing are our battle-grounds. We fight against our own inefficiencies and bugs; we fight our competitors. We will win, as we are better than others. We are stronger, more highly skilled, and more disciplined!"

Grim-faced brave soldiers jumped from one slide of his deck to another. Swords clanged, arrows whizzed, and soldiers' teeth grinded. The room smelt of gun-powder.

Our own Manoj, just appointed to manage Evo delivery, presented right after Dong-Ju. He conveyed our desire to help others and work for them so calmly and clearly that the room filled with the sweet and delicate scent of lotus flowers.

But after Dong-Ju's forceful performance, Manoj's PowerPoint full of smiling cartoon characters made us MCR India look spineless. I didn't like how the short, stern Korean leader was looking down on the taller Manoj, as if telling him, "Peaceful Indian yogis can do nothing against the tough Korean martial artists!"

Now, a few years later, I should have felt triumphant — the Tao Te Ching is right. "The soft overcomes the hard; the gentle overcomes the rigid" — work from "hard" Korea eventually flows to "soft" India.

Except that under the camouflage of military metaphors and immaculate black suits, Dong-Ju turned out to be a real gentleman and a strong professional. It was a pleasure working with him. He and Manoj got along extremely well, always going out during our corporate conferences for a smoke together. It wasn't the fault of this tough warrior that the heavy gears of corporate karma had turned that way.

Now Dong-Ju, already laid off, was trying to convince his ex-employees to help us in India, in memory of the good old days.

Developers and the Exodus

The developers' paradise that we were building was a middle managers' hell — by design. Power had to shift towards those who produced value. All others should serve them.

I was subconsciously modelling my engineers' Garden of Eden after the lost paradise of Lufthansa's first class. Only instead of lobsters, caviar, and roasted pigeons, we promised autonomy, purpose, mastery, flat hierarchy, and fast career progression. The moon and the stars remained the same.

The problem was, the developers did not want to enter our sublime paradise. They were quite comfortable where they were. Maslow's pyramid proved much less attractive to climb than the pyramid of corporate hierarchy.

The Bible says that after God freed the Jewish people

from slavery in Egypt and gave them the Tablets of the Law, the people had to wander in the harsh desert for forty years. It takes time to get rid of the habits of slavery.

The Jewish people were not even too keen on the promised land. Rather, they longed for Egypt, complaining and rebelling at every opportunity. This is so understandable — slavery provides the best job security and a pot of meat once a week. Independence and freedom are desirable when they are absent but tough to live with. As the saying goes, it was easier to get the Israelites out of Egypt than Egypt out of the Israelites. It was easier to switch to a new operating model than to squeeze the authoritarian culture out of people's minds. The thick blood of command-and-control ran deep in developers' veins.

Our teams were supposed to be like driverless cars. Every attempt by a "leader" to grab the steering wheel or push the car was punished by hard-hearted coaches. Jack's Zen ruler whistled in the air. But the developers were in no hurry to get behind the wheel — they could not believe that the bosses refused to "manage" them.

"Can crocodiles become vegetarians?" a developer asked me. Good question. Even for a caterpillar, it is not easy to turn into a beautiful butterfly. But how do you become a butterfly if you are a middle-aged crocodile?

Engineers began testing their superiors to see if they

would keep their promises and allow teams to make decisions. Nothing like trial-and-error. Our first three self-managed teams got together and made their first decision — to reorganize back into a component structure with a waterfall process. Either they were just teasing and testing us, the leadership, or they sincerely thought that the old ways were more efficient.

Most likely, both.

We didn't have forty years or even forty days to wander in the desert. I had to clarify, "There are rules for freedom. Learn them first, change later."

Developers and Naked Monks

I've always been a proponent of private ownership and personal responsibility. Many years ago, my late brother — a poet, a math teacher, and a natural-born businessman — sold a massive, elaborately decorated fountain to a Soviet collective farm, a kolkhoz. Such a trifle as the complete lack of water supply to their collective farm did not bother them at all. Since then, I don't trust "collective responsibility" or "the wisdom of the masses" — I've seen collective indifference and insanity too often.

Therefore, we always clearly defined who the boss was. Who was the one throat to choke, as Manoj liked to say. Not to choke this throat, as tempting as it often was, but to mark the boundaries of personal responsibility. Poorly drawn borders often become the main cause of conflicts, be it corporate or geopolitical, including the Indo-Pakistani and the Indo-Chinese.

The new model clearly defined who did what, when, and, most importantly, why. But this time, I bet on the "collective," not the "personal." The code in an adaptive organization belongs to everyone and to no one personally. Individual achievements and acts of corporate heroism are symptoms of systemic failures, not reasons to celebrate. If a Ram Kumar fixed the bug at two o'clock in the morning, where were the others? Why was this bug allowed to creep in to begin with?

Contributions to the success of the team matter; individual achievements do not. Someone who serves tea to the team may be more valuable than a Superman writing brilliant code but killing everyone else's motivation to work.

An adaptive team reminds me of the naked Jain monks. Jainism is an ancient religion, rooted in Hinduism, but quite distinct. It takes non-attachment to extremes: Jain monks have no worldly possessions, not even clothing. Several times I saw them hurrying about their business nearby the sacred hill of Shravanabelagola — completely naked. They can't spend more than one night in the same place to prevent getting emotionally attached. Attachment, whether physical or emotional, to a nice person or a cosy cot, blocks the path to liberation and enlightenment.

Attachment is what egos have, naturally. Isn't an ego itself just a point where multiple attachments intersect?

Adaptive organizations, like ancient traditions, are not ego-friendly.

You can't make a career in an adaptive organization. You can't climb a corporate pyramid — it is flat. You can't win a Big Corporate Carrot Race — there is no race. Developers have nothing to own (not even the source code), nothing to hide (not even the project status), and nothing to get attached to (not even their careers). There are no intermediaries — priests or managers — between the egoless teams and their true gods, the customers.

In legacy organizations, long development cycles are calm and serene — until a plus-sized lady sings, and pre-release fever sets in. Then heroes and leaders are born from the corporate swamp all by themselves, like toads from the ancient Nile silt. When the release is done, there is a lull again.

But in an adaptive team, you can't relax, as the next release is always in two shakes of a lamb's tail. Like, always.

Owning nothing, never stopping, the team is always ahead of itself, always in the flow: in the next feature, towards the next delivery, improving with each sprint. Working in such an organization is certainly not for everyone. For strong "individual achievers" and "free spirits" like me, this ain't Nirvana.

Still I was hoping that of all people, Subhash would like it...

Subhash Plays Bach

Subhash delicately entered my room. He was so polite and courteous that he seemed to be made of soft suede.

Subhash was from Calcutta — the last stronghold of the Indian intelligentsia. It is also a bastion of authentic Russian culture. Subhash knew much more about Russian history than I did (which, on second thought, was not that difficult). He had a deep, delicate, Russian soul, so I was always surprised that he didn't speak Russian. Instead, like most Indians, he spoke four or five Indian languages and English. Subhash's English was richer than Shakespeare's, as it also included software terminology, which Shakespeare probably did not know.

When Subhash joined MCR, I was sure I had found a "chosen one" who would one day become my successor. But his career didn't take off. I almost dragged him along the management path by force. He resisted as politely, as stubbornly.

"I'm not Homo Corporaticus," said Subhash. "I don't trust bureaucratic machines and management. I don't like them."

Subhash preferred to stick to the working class and write Java code. The very word "management" sounded from his lips like the name of a contagious disease. After enunciating it, Subhash looked as if he urgently had to rinse his mouth.

The lack of desire to be the boss would make Subhash the perfect boss — a meta-manager. I tried to convince him that meta-managers are like poets: they rhyme people in a team like words in a poem. They are orchestra conductors.

I had only one trait in common with Moses — neither of us was good at convincing people. Subhash came by to thank me and say goodbye.

"I've always respected and liked you, Subhash. Perhaps more than you've liked me. I'm so sorry you're leaving now, as we're rebuilding the organization. I thought you'd love it. By the way, where are you heading?"

"I don't know yet, Vladi ... I talked it over with my wife and decided that I would be better off on my own. I want to try myself as a freelancer."

"What can I say... Good luck to you! And please keep sending me your Bach recordings."

A year ago, Subhash decided to learn to play Bach and asked me to introduce him to a Russian piano teacher living in Bangalore. Since then, Subhash had been sending me his monthly progress reports — MP3 recordings.

Subhash's departure hurt like the loss of one of the notes in our musical score or one of the colours of our rainbow. Still, Subhash was a soloist, not a manager-conductor, and not the third violin of an engineering orchestra. He was an individual player, a virtuoso. We'd started a team game, like curling.

It was not for him.

Looked like it fit Akash much better...

Boss' Effigy

Akash, a former project manager newly converted into a Product Owner, walked into my glass fish tank. After a ritual exchange of pleasantries, he opened up his heart.

"You know, Vladi, Evo is not in a good place. People are leaving. They do not believe in our future. They don't trust you! And you are still surrounded by the same old clique. You are out of touch with reality, as your gang does not let you see the truth!"

I was a little taken aback. On the one hand, I liked his frankness. On the other hand, I'd rather start my day with a more inspiring message.

"Um ... Could you please tell me the truth, Akash?"

Akash didn't need to think it over — he looked well

prepared for the meeting.

"Honestly, Vladi, I don't think you are a good leader!"

He didn't want to hurt me; he was just testing the boundaries of his new freedom, I told myself. And at the same time, he was tasting my blood. Looked like he liked both. No, I am not going to be offended!

Being of sound and disposing mind and memory and not acting under any fraud, menace, duress, or undue influence, I gave up my authority. I've brought it on myself. I didn't want to be a "leader" — now I had to live with the consequences.

"Akash, thank you for being open. I really appreciate your trust. I mean it!"

We talked over several issues that were important to Akash. Understandably, he mentioned the lack of recognition and the insufficient remuneration for his hard work. But mostly, he wanted to talk about my clique and me.

According to corporate folklore, Japan has special "anger rooms" where employees vent their frustrations by pummelling their bosses' plastic doubles or effigies. Listening to Akash, I felt like my own effigy in the anger room. I wished I was made of plastic — it would probably hurt less.

It was too much for me. Besides, why let him spoil his karma like that?

"I really appreciate your openness, Akash. But don't

you think that a little compassion towards us — imperfect leaders — would make sense? We're human too, aren't we?"

Akash was not so sure. He was like a teenager who found the key to his parents' wine cellar. Only when he had drunk the last bottle to the bottom did he leave the room.

"Our guys need to feel free, not scared of managers! What Akash did was right for him. Besides, I'm not a hundred-dollar bill to be liked by everyone!" I kept telling myself.

That night was surprisingly quiet. There was a power cut, and even the cicadas and night birds were silent, as if they were also unplugged from the universal power supply. The silence was broken only by the screams of a maddened water pump, sucking electricity out of thin air. The wounded pump filled the universe with its high-pitched squeals, full of anguish and pain, till midnight. And, by morning, the house was left without water.

I hardly slept that night. And the next day I had to deal with yet another rebellion.

An Angel in the Boardroom

Twelve teams working together for our biggest customer, with more than ten million subscribers, decided to go home at four-thirty in the afternoon every day. A reasonable balance between work and personal life is one of the pillars of Agile, isn't it? As for the deadline, it was not their problem. Let the explosive customer — Paul, the expat CTO — balance on the verge of a nervous breakdown.

Murali, our chief architect, was fuming.

"These guys are lazy! They are, like, making fun of us!"

What do you do when a dozen self-driving teams drive confidently towards the edge of a cliff? In the ideal, Agile world, I should enjoy the view until they "fail small" and learn their lessons. In the real world, they were going to fall into an abyss, not onto a trampoline. If this project failed, I could turn the lights off and go home.

Still, I couldn't do anything, as the teams' "wise" decision did not violate the rules of our operating model.

I had already used my power to impose the rules of the game. When the game was on, I had to play by the rules — and I didn't like it. But if I made an exception and switched to command-and-control at the first sign of problems, my exceptions would become the rules. The Grand Canyon of corporate hypocrisy begins with a small crack between what the bosses expect from others and what they do themselves.

If I issued an executive order now, I could forget about the cultural change and the flying boat. Teams would get coveted proof that they couldn't trust managers and would switch their brains into an energy-saving mode.

But if I didn't do anything, it would be a disaster.

I asked Jack, our coach, for permission to meet with key people from these teams. I didn't know exactly what to tell them; I thought I'd play it by ear.

Entering the meeting, I felt out of place — a stranger in my native boardroom. I was used to my people depending on me. I had no experience depending on them.

We started, as usual, with a polite discussion of the weather and last night's cricket match. I shouldn't have been in a hurry, but extended small talk isn't my forte. I went straight to business.

"Look, guys, I made a promise: you decide how you work. Now the fate of this project is in your hands. If we fail and the client goes to competitors, Evo will be shut down, and I will lose my job. If you think the shortest path to success is to close the shop at four-thirty every day, so be it. I will leave the office together with you every day, in the spirit of solidarity. But I beg of you, please think of the consequences!"

Everyone kept silent. I was ill at ease. Maybe they mistook my speech for cheap emotional blackmail? In a sense, it was...

"So, what do you guys think?"

Silence.

I looked pointedly at Jack the Ripper of Managers, intensely winking with my third eye. Jack didn't utter a word, grinning tenderly and carnivorously, not even trying to conceal his delight...

I addressed the team again. They still kept their mouths zipped.

After several minutes of awkward silence, I had no choice. With a hollow smile marking me as a bleeding but proud character, I headed for the door. I felt betrayed by those I worked for. I showed my vulnerability and got punched by their silence — right in my solar plexus. What kind of people were they?

Actually, no point in blaming them — I had made a fool of myself, inventing these stupid "management models."

I slowly turned the doorknob. One more step and I'd drown in the dark abyss of the corridor to never return. This was how my Indian journey was going to end.

"Vladi, sir, please come back, sir," someone suddenly uttered.

I had never heard a voice as sweet and delightful. Soaring up to the ceiling, I flew across the room back to our long oval corporate table.

People around the table gradually started opening up. They were scared, annoyed, and confused, which was absolutely normal for a transformation.

Turned out, the managers from the client's side made

it very difficult for our teams. They swore, scolded, and put pressure. Even Jack's ruler broke on them. I had not interfered earlier, not wanting to irritate our largest customer. Only now had I realized how important for my teams it was. Akash was right after all — I relied too much on coaches and directors. I knew the realities, but I did not feel them.

This had to change.

There were other issues. Teams were upset that the management did nothing about the hardware delays. Actually, we did everything we could. Paul — the customer's CTO — was screaming at the Chinese vendor every day. Not that it helped, but still, our people should know we were trying.

The scars of integration with Leviathan were also aching. People had questions about their career paths. Interestingly, everyone was convinced I had already submitted my resignation.

"Don't you even dream of it — you guys have to bear with me for longer!"

It was the first time that we were talking like equals, even though I was a Big Foreign Boss, a "Sir," twice the age of the oldest of them. The teams promised to do everything they could. There was no mention of a four-thirty-in-the-afternoon end of business anymore.

I can still feel the chill of that metal doorknob. Thank God I didn't open the door!

Later I tried to find that sweet-voiced engineer to give him a hug for saving me. Curiously, no one remembered him. Maybe it was a visit from my guardian angel — in the form of a young chubby engineer.

Top Managers and Greek Philosophers

Engineers believe that their leaders live in ivory towers, detached from the harsh realities of delivery. Most often they are right.

Before our transformation, I used to climb out of my fishbowl once in a while to go out for lunch with a randomly selected victim from my staff. We'd talk of cabbages and kings, and problems in our own kingdom, so I thought I knew pretty well what was going on.

Instead of talking to someone once a week, I had to talk with teams every day. So my directors and I stepped out of our ivory towers for daily walks in our development paddies, where our engineers work so hard. We strolled across our spacious office, one by one, or in pairs, like peripatetic Greek philosophers, admiring the Scrum boards and talking to people.

The walls and columns of our office were decorated with Indian tribal art. The Madhubani and Warli murals were so wise, naive, and beautiful that my heart ached sweetly. Looking at them, I realized that simplicity is deeper than sophistication. Minimalism is more abundant than redundancy. And innovation results from following tradition.

Our Scrum boards, decorated with diagrams and Post-It™ notes like Christmas trees, hung next to the murals. Scrum boards were the modest contribution of our software tribe to the art of the other Indian tribes.

Scrum rituals, similar to religious practices, are linked to physical objects. As a typical nerd, I do not trust the physical world — and this distrust is mutual. But even I had to admit, when we write on small Post-It™ notes, we wrote crisply and clearly, so that the message "stuck." When dealing with physical objects, your body is at work, not just your mind. Understanding is not only in the brain but also in the bones and muscles.

Conversations usually started around the "obstacle list" — a list of issues preventing the team from being faster. Anything from dependencies in the delivery pipeline to food to parking issues. If the engineering manager and Scrum Master were unable to remove the obstacle, they passed it on to my directors. If the directors failed, the obstacle bubbled up to me automatically, in just two days. I had to explain to the engineers what I had done and where I'd gotten stuck. I was accountable to my team, so I had to master the bitter craft of apology.

"I'm sorry, I called up Israel again, but their module is delayed. We'll have to work with the simulator for a little longer."

"I'm sorry, but Dong-Ju could convince only five out of the seventy-five laid-off Korean engineers to stay for a month. We are urgently sending our developers to Seoul for the knowledge transfer."

"I'm sorry, I know you spend hours in traffic jams at the Technopark exit. I get stuck there every day, too. We've spoken to the Technopark manager and threatened to delay the rent. He was as slippery as a fish in water, telling me it was above his pay grade. Only municipal authorities and political parties can help! Anyway, we will keep putting pressure on him until we get it resolved!"

I could relate to that Technopark boss. My VP rank was also insufficient — most impediments were settling in my personal obstacles list, like shipwrecks in the Sargasso Sea. Most of them, such as cross-site dependencies, could only be resolved at the ecosystem level. Some required Sandra's attention. Others, the Leviathan president's and the UN Secretary General's.

In the meantime, non-doing was hard. Instead of discussing delays and shuffling "resources" between projects, we had to listen to the teams and help them where they needed it, not where it was convenient for us to help them.

Wraiths in Delivery Pipelines

Once, walking through the corporate paddies, Manoj and I started talking with a DevOps engineer — and got stuck for a couple of hours, watching a piece of code going through our delivery pipeline. It's one thing to look at Vijay's diagram in the conference room. It's another thing to sit next to an engineer and feel his pain: the complete build process took forty-three minutes. We had to reduce the time from "code commit," when the engineer submits the new code, till the moment the test results are ready.

Vijay organized a hackathon and announced: for every minute saved, the winning team would get ten thousand rupees (about US$150).

By the end of the twenty-four-hour hackathon, the sleepy, red-eyed winners had reduced the build time from forty-three to seven minutes. We achieved more in one day than in a few years!

The finance department was trying to find the budget category for the bonus payout. The amount was petty, especially compared to the savings from the build time reduction. But there was no such budget category as "hackathon bonuses," so we got stuck. The finance department had to launch a hackathon of its own, to bend the rules.

Anyway, our pipeline had become much faster. The test automation system had stabilized; its coverage exceeded 80 percent — and it had started bringing in real value. Engineers realized that test automation was not a corporate tax but a useful tool.

We already had more than forty customers. When developers submitted new code for their customers, they could break other customers' projects. Previously, the developers hadn't cared about other components. Now they didn't care about other customers. "Other guys should test it — it's their headache!"

Monitors showing the state of the code trunk glowed an alarming crimson instead of a boring green. Well, let them glow...

How do we make our engineers hear us? — Literally!

Vijay fetched a fire engine siren from somewhere and connected it to his delivery pipeline. Try not to hear it now! When the code trunk broke in one of the projects, our siren emitted a sad, soul-rending howl, like a pack of wraiths at the sight of a delicious hobbit. Developers rushed to fix the trunk. It groaned and bent, but no longer broke under the weight of hundreds of code submissions per day.

Applause in the Boardroom

It's amazing how much you can learn by simply looking at a Scrum board.

"Why does your burndown chart look like a cliff, not a staircase? Do you have dependencies? Are graphic designers late again? Or maybe your user stories are not sliced thin enough? Or perhaps you just postponed testing till the last minute at the end of the sprint?"

We managers were only allowed to ask questions. For giving wise but unsolicited advice and instructions, we could get a beating — nothing like a Zen ruler to curb the best intentions.

"Oh, the release burnup chart is not converging. How is our friend Paul doing? Is he very angry?"

Paul — the acrimonious CTO of our biggest Indian customer — was angry as hell. Though his people had formally agreed to switch to the adaptive model, they kept working with us using the good old toothpaste principle: the harder you squeeze the tube, the more you get.

Our roles while dealing with Paul were well defined. First, Manoj started his sweet aria — he promised Paul to do everything in his power to deliver on time. Then our teams' chorus entered the scene with a heroic hymn. The final tragic theme of the last act was mine: "My apologies, Paul, it will never happen again."

Then the cycle repeated itself.

By that time, Shalini had already finished our operating model rollout. Her Latin American customers were quite happy, so I suggested that overloaded Manoj pass the pleasure of dealing with Paul to Shalini. This potato was so hot that Manoj agreed to drop it, without even asking for compensation.

Shalini spent two weeks with the teams, non-stop. And then Paul summoned her to his den in Delhi. There, Paul scolded, berated, and shouted for forty minutes without a break. The entire thesaurus was not enough to describe his fury. When he finally got a bit winded, Shalini calmly explained the complexities of this critical release. Our contract, signed long ago in the Neolithic age, defined the dates, scope of work, and cost. Nothing could be worse than such a contract for adaptive delivery, but changing it would take a century or two.

"So," Shalini concluded judiciously, "you can't fool yourself: the team's performance is known; it's written on the Scrum board, in 'story points.' No matter how much pressure you put on the engineers, we will not deliver all the functionality on time. But I would really appreciate it, Paul, if you personally prioritize our user stories."

Paul's jaw dropped as he stared at Shalini. No one had ever spoken to him like that in the super-polite India.

"And one more thing," Shalini added in a soft, almost motherly voice. "Your people allow themselves to raise voice at developers. Maybe you are the role model for them. But this is wrong, Paul — these are your teams. If your people want to, let them yell at me, not at the engineers."

Paul muttered something unintelligible.

Shortly after, Paul's people stopped throwing tantrums.

Several weeks passed; the teams went home at four-thirty — not in the afternoon, as they had planned, but in the morning. Still, no matter how hard they tried, they could not complete everything on time. Luckily, it turned out that "everything" was not even needed. When we had been late in the predictive waterfall paradigm, nothing was ready for delivery towards the deadline — we were still tearing through the thickets of integration. Now all the features prioritized by Paul were working. He agreed that we would deliver other, deprioritized features later. Or maybe never — market needs might change.

Paul and his people came over to Bangalore, summoned all teams working for them — and gave them a standing ovation.

The cake they brought was not all that tasty, but

the corporate boardroom looked like La Scala opera house.

Customers and Love

Success is contagious, like coronavirus. I no longer had to tap-dance my usual excuses in front of the customers.

Engineers in legacy organizations are like cogs hidden deep inside giant mechanical guts. They live in different layers of reality than their customers, meeting them as often as fairies or unicorns.

Previously, rare Evo clients who managed to reach Bangalore interacted with their teams under the watchful eye of account managers. Without their supervision, developers could blurt out something wrong to the customer. Like the truth.

Now the customers were on our side; they were part of the team. And they were the ones who defined what teams did.

Account managers were appalled. Instead of sending status reports as optimistic and enthusiastic as pre-election speeches, we gave the customers full access to virtual Scrum boards — copies of physical ones. Radical transparency was shocking. The naked truth, not even covered by the thin veil of "managing customer expectations," was visible and accessible to everyone.

The customers were our gods, but both gods and humans had to play by the rules of the playbook. There is a story about a Jewish community that sued God Almighty in a religious court. People fulfilled their part of the contract and followed his Law to the letter, while God kept bestowing calamities and suffering upon them. Even God is not above his Law. Nor are the customers above the laws of Scrum.

A long time ago, to create a flow of work into India, we had handed over Indian teams to our internal customers. Foreign managers ended up as victims of a "reverse Stockholm syndrome," feeling empathy for the Indian programmers whom they had taken hostage. Now it was the same story with the customers. They had gulped the bait of authority over "their" teams — and swallowed the fishhook of taking responsibility. And that created the right conditions for love.

It was a déjà vu when one of the customers told me, "I don't really like working with India, but my team in Bangalore is an exception."

Sure — "my Indians are better than yours!"

Some Like It Hot

I've heard many times that building an Agile adaptive organization in the hierarchical and command-and-control-ish India is next to impossible.

We took a risk — and after splitting the hard and shaggy shell of hierarchy, found the sweet pulp of teamwork and self-management.

Teamwork is in the cultural DNA of India; when authorities are not very efficient, people rely on each other to survive. In rural areas, when elephants encroach on fields, neighbours team up to chase them away. Buses and trains are so packed that you can't get in and hold on without a dozen helping hands. Every day you trust your life, not just your code, to others.

In a city, anything can happen, too. A water pump bursting, a fire, a flood, the incursion of a monkey gang or a giant cobra. Self-management and autonomy? Every residential complex in India, including mine, is a small fort well equipped to withstand an alien invasion, with its own power generator, gym, and swimming pool. Water is gathered, recycled, and reused.

Privacy? Who needs it! Everyone knows what you cook for dinner, what your kids' grades at school are, and what your last row with your mother-in-law was about. But when you need help, your neighbours always come to your rescue.

Every day, citizens of the Exotica Prestige apartment complex where I lived teamed up against forces of nature and municipal mismanagement. Bangalore is drying up, so a retired civil engineer dealt with water supply. A nice auntie took care of garbage segregation.

A young engineer looked after a coughing elderly electric generator. Someone stepped out of the fort to regulate traffic jams on the local roads, in the absence of cops. Any new tenant in the building was immediately entwined in this benevolent and elastic Indranet.

This experience was also evident in the office. People worked smoothly in self-managed teams. But as soon as their superiors appeared, life froze — the engineers fell into a stupor. Seniority was respected — for good and for bad.

Both command-and-control and adaptive paradigms can work in India. They just can't work together. It is either this way or that way. Boiling-hot or ice-cold, India is definitely not lukewarm.

The Flying Boat

Within a year, our entire organization had switched to the adaptive paradigm. Our bet on frequent releases, collective code ownership, and self-managed teams working directly with customers turned out to be the winning one.

We reduced the staff by almost half, from more than a thousand Evo engineers to 650. Other departments also bled people, so my entire centre shrank from almost 2,500 employees to hardly 1,500.

Letting people go improved neither my spirits nor

my karma. But the remaining team was twice as efficient, so we were able to extend Evo's footprint to 80 million households around the globe.

Our American coach, Jack the Ripper of Managers, told us that this was his best transformation experience in a lifetime.

Following Alex's advice — "smoke and fly" — we built an organization without leaders. Even Alex himself acknowledged it, "Vladi, your rather ordinary developers do absolutely extraordinary stuff." That was music to my ears, more than I could ever expect from an Eastern European.

Since our acquisition, I'd had seven reporting managers changed within a year and a half. It felt like speed dating. I was hardly introduced to a new boss — Bibbidi-Bobbidi-Boo... Puff! — and they were gone.

Seventh time was the charm. My last (and the best) Californian boss came over to Bangalore to see for himself what exactly we were doing here. After technical discussions during the day and a good drink (or two, maybe three or four) with the team in the evening, he muttered, as if surprised at his own words, "You know, guys, I think I like what you are doing here! And I like you...."

What else could I strive for, after achieving my goals and getting some harsh and quite unexpected corporate love?

Just one thing — an official confirmation of our success.

Leviathan Inc. announced our legacy Evo as their next-generation platform for Satellite TV. The new Neo platform could not catch up with our old legacy Evo and was terminated.

The world of software development is spinning like a crazy merry-go-round:

- We develop a brand-new system.
- We contaminate it with poor maintenance.
- We send it to software Varanasi in India to die.
- We write a new system from a clean slate.

The carousel keeps turning round and round — but we were able to get off.

There is an old joke about a couple with a child. The child falls into a puddle and gets up, covered in mud. Dad asks Mom, "Shall we clean up this one, or should we make a new one?"

In the West, developers love making new ones. This approach is undeniably pleasurable but not necessarily the most efficient. As for us, we have learned to "clean up" legacy software and make it better than the new one, mastering the beautiful Zen of continuous maintenance.

Ta-dah.

CONCLUSION. THE WAY OF HEAVEN

Happiness and Mosquitoes

We — the three directors and I — were sitting on the terrace of a Bangalore restaurant in the semi-darkness. We were fighting off Indian mosquitoes, as stealthy as F-35s, as we were drinking and chatting about Life, the Universe, and Leviathan.

"Yossi sends his warmest regards to you. I spoke with him yesterday. In the business of transformation, he is so much ahead of us: our former boss has become... you'd never guess! An interior designer! He is already flooded with orders. Yossi is so happy that I envy him!"

For a while, we discussed the intrinsic connections between product architecture, organization design, and interior design.

"Are you happy at work, Vladi?" Manoj asked suddenly. "What makes you happy?"

To get to these types of questions in the West, you

need to drink a lot more. In India, you can get to this point with just a coke — teenage questions flutter in the air of India like fireflies.

"Hey, I'm not going to reply alone! Let everybody answer. Why don't we start with you, Manoj?"

Manoj pondered for a moment, his soulful, aristocratic profile swaying in tune with the frogs' chorus.

"Happiness... I'd like to retire early and live a simple life in the countryside. I would teach the children in the village school during the day. Towards evening, I would sit under a big Banyan tree with a glass of good Scotch, enjoying the sunset and teaching people gathered around me words of wisdom."

What a beautiful picture of happiness — so far removed from the realities of today. Manoj was struggling. Everything he believed in at work — personal responsibility, clarity of structure, delegation — had gone for a toss, as he says. The organization he built over the years had been dismantled. His subordinates and friends had been left behind. Manoj tried his best to adapt to the new approach, but it was not his cup of tea.

"But, Manoj, you can be happy at work too! You already have hundreds of followers in your office, and I'm one of them. As for sunsets, there is always some software sent to 'sunset' in India, as they say. And we never lack good Scotch!"

The incessant chorus of invisible frogs was so loud

that the air around us boiled like dark masala tea in the huge pot of night.

"What about you, Padma?"

"Well, that's a simple question. Money makes me happy. You know, Vladi! Tons of money!"

Padma wouldn't be Padma if she didn't tease us as always. With our transformation, she also changed. She cooled down, become more tolerant — and her technical talents shined even brighter.

Shalini was the only one left.

"Sure... I guess I'm happy when I make others happy. When I take care of others and they feel good."

Had someone else said it, it would have sounded fake. But Shalini was pathologically sincere. When teams and people (including me) lost direction and meaning, she was always there to help. Shalini once told me she would like to establish a new religion of humanism one day. Schools, orphanages, and hospitals would become the sacred places of this religion. Serving people would be serving God.

"But, hey, our office is a bit of a kindergarten, a bit of a school. It fits your definition of a sacred place, doesn't it?"

"True. A woman learns multitasking, time management, and patience at home — and applies them at work," Shalini slightly shifted the conversation.

I was surprised: was the office really more important

to her than home?!

"No, both are equally important. But it's easier for me to do something good for others at work — I have authority here. It is very different at home."

In traditional, male-dominated Indian society, families are still run by women. But women lead from behind. Every decision a woman makes should look as if it is taken by her all-powerful in-laws or by her husband, who naively considers himself to be the master of the house. This soft power — the uniquely Indian female art of managing from behind — is closest to the future leadership model I'm looking for.

Not surprisingly, when we redefined management, women took the lead. They have turned into excellent Scrum Masters, architects, Product Owners — Jarna, Roopa, Lakshmi, Bharati, Mani, Nalini, and many others.

Padma suddenly became serious — one of her trademark mood swings.

"You know, I don't believe in making others happy anymore. I want to have time for myself. But I was taught to take care of others from my childhood. Now, when I do something for myself, I feel guilty, and I don't know how to stop it."

Padma is on a continuous quest for meaning and purpose, always trying to surpass herself. Sometimes she goes in a direction opposite to Shalini's. Everyone, as Manoj likes to put it, has their own karma.

A shooting star drew a line in the dark velvet of the sky. Again, I missed the opportunity to make a wish.

"Padma, do you remember when we sat with you and Surendra in a cafe in Tel-Aviv? Surendra shouted, 'Look! Look! A shooting star!' It was the size of a coin, huge, completely alive, green and gold. I made a wish... And then it turned out to be the Israeli missile defence system that shot down a rocket from Gaza. Literally a shooting star."

"Come on, Vladi, don't change the subject," Manoj shook his finger at me. "What makes you happy? Spill the beans!"

"Um... come to think of it... I am happy when I am free of my own self. When I write... or when I am in love... or when I watch Theyyam... When my work goes well. Yes, I am happy when I am carried away by the flow. When the 'I' gets dissolved in the current, like a sugar cube in a cup of tea."

"Vladi, you always give us philosophical lectures when we talk about simple things," Padma laughs, her huge black eyes sparkling in the dark. "Admit it, this is what makes you happy!"

I did.

I was happy at work despite all the troubles, and I was happy with my team. I used to think we were the four elements, fire, water, earth, and air. No, I was probably the fifth element — the ether, the void, the space for other things. My role of a meta-manager was not to "be" but to create space for these three and for all our engineers to feel happy, to learn, and to have fun.

With or without me.

Our dinner was over, and Shalini hurried back home. Padma and Manoj were going for a drink to a dance bar. Hmm... they had forgotten to invite me. My dance seemed to be coming to an end.

I strolled towards the car, where faithful Rajesh the driver was waiting for me.

The Way of Heaven

I've heard that in medieval Japan, artists at the peak of success had to leave everything behind. To prove their skills, they had to start afresh, under a different name in a different city. I didn't want to change my name, and I didn't have any skills to prove. Still, this chapter of my life was ending.

A few tears were shed during my emotional farewell party, as expected. But, to my secret disappointment, the show was going on smoothly without me. There was no time for nostalgia, as the next release was always in less than two shakes of a lamb's tail, less than a fortnight.

It was evident to me who should take the helm of our flying boat, but not everyone accepted Shalini filling my shoes. It was especially tough for Manoj. He was an experienced manager, Shalini's senior in both age and rank. He was my "number two" for many years. Besides, it is not easy for an Indian man to report to a woman, and even more so, to a younger one.

Shalini and I really wanted him to stay — Evo with Manoj is much better than Evo without Manoj.

I packed my modest stuff, settled over the years in my office, like the sediment of time. A few photos, a few documents, and a clay figurine of Ganesha with a laptop.

I used to say we needed developers, not gods. It took me years to realize what I had already known: engineers who create worlds with the words of programming languages are our true gods. We managers are not the Agni Theyyam performers. We are those inconspicuous people who dress performers up, beat out the rhythm on our drums, and bring them whiskey. Most importantly, we hold mirrors. Looking into them and becoming self-aware, our "ordinary" Indian developers reveal the ancient software gods and goddesses inside their minds. Then they work miracles, throw themselves into the heart of the corporate flame, release a product without bugs every two weeks, and dance on burning coals.

Lord Ganesha at the keyboard is no paradox. "Sacred" and "mundane," "personal" and "professional" are the same. Being a corporate manager demands personal efforts like those of a Buddhist monk in a monastery. Taming your mind, coping with negative emotions, and keeping your cool is also required at boring corporate meetings or when dealing with irritating bosses and subordinates.

My friend's friend, a New Yorker, had become a Buddhist monk in India and worked hard for twenty years to transform himself. But when he returned to New York, his old irritation and desperation made a quick comeback too, as if those twenty years in a monastery were a dream.

For us managers, the office is our ashram. No wonder I heard an angel in the corporate boardroom.

Our business suits (and Agile jeans) are saffron robes in disguise.

PowerPoint presentations are our holy scriptures.

And our team is the true Sangha (Buddhist community of learning). We are Indra-net nodes, reflecting each other. Maybe there are no "us," just infinite reflections of reflections.

Better to stop short than fill to the brim.

Retire when the work is done. This is the way of heaven.

My stuff collected over many years was not enough to fill even one cardboard box to the brim. I go light (with my Google Drive storage packed to the last bit, heh-heh).

Hair of the Spirit

"This is what happened to my friend's father," said Rajesh as we were stuck in traffic on our way home from the office — for the last time.

"This man had a sugar cane field and a farm where jaggery — unrefined cane sugar — was made. One night, this man heard a noise coming from the field. He thought someone was robbing him, but when he stepped out, he saw that spirits were working in his field. Work was in full swing; fire was burning in the furnace. The spirits looked exactly like people, only they were completely naked. This man immediately stripped his clothes and mixed with the spirits. He worked with them. He tasted the jaggery they cooked. 'No mortal could brew such a delightful jaggery,' he said later.

"Before dawn, the spirits started to slowly disappear. Then this man, my friend's father, pulled a hair out of the head of one little spirit, tied it in a knot, and hid it. He knew that if you snatch a hair from a ghost, it will become your servant and will fulfil all your wishes.

"The next evening, this spirit came to that man and pleaded with him, 'Give me my hair back, set me free!' But the man did not listen to the spirit.

"So the spirit lived in the man's house like his son; he worked, helped, and served. He lived there for many years. And when his master died, the spirit disappeared at the same moment."

As for me, not just one hair, but all of them were left here, so India won't let me go.

"I myself was in that field," said Rajesh. "And I drank the water of twenty-one coconuts there; I could not stop, so delicious it was! But then my stomach ached so much that I could not walk; I suffered a lot, sir!"

Ganesha's figurine might get damaged in the cardboard box on this broken road, so I held it in my hands. The world is sliding faster and faster into an online computer-based reality. But Sri Ganesha — the wise "remover of obstacles," as he is called — is there for us. Plunging into his laptop, the divine Scrum Master and meta-manager comes to our rescue — online.

OM GAM GANAPATAYE NAMAHA SHARANAM GANESHA

Life After Life

This story began for me on an LH754 flight to India, so it should have ended on the return flight LH755. But life is not subject to the laws of the genre. You think it's a full stop. Then another one comes along. And another one... Unexpectedly, the full stop becomes a dot-dot-dot of an ellipsis...

This is what happened to our MCR Ltd. In an almost

impossible twist of fate, it has been spat out by Leviathan as an independent company under a new name. Ron, our wise CEO who orchestrated the spin-off and buy-out, is now acting as its Executive Chairman, raising our cash cow from the dead to a bright new life.

Time is cyclical in India. The same word "kal" means both "yesterday" and "tomorrow" in Hindi, depending on the context. Life ends in death no more than death ends in life.

The ancient Greek sage Heraclitus said, "No man steps into the same river twice." If he knew Ron, he'd think twice.

Our Rajesh the driver is no longer a driver, but a Manager — office administration. Rajesh is a great friend of our former coach, Jack the Ripper of Managers. They travel together to ashrams and make pilgrimages to holy places all across India. From time to time, Rajesh sends me spiritual quotes on WhatsApp, which (penitent sigh) I seldom read.

Jack the Ripper of Managers works in India. He is confident that the heavy authoritarian, hierarchical structures are alien to India and were imposed by the conquerors — the Mughals, and then the Brits. India is self-organizing chaos. Applying simple principles to achieve complex results is an ancient Indian tradition.

Once a month, Jack and Rajesh go on a pilgrimage around the sacred mountain in Tiruvannamalai, among tens of thousands of other devotees who organize and manage themselves perfectly well — without any police or officials around. So all we need to do is to let people solve problems for themselves, Jack thinks. I wish he were right.

Padma left Leviathan shortly after me. Now she heads the development centre of one of the most innovative companies in the world. I knew this would happen when I first saw her at the computer, years ago, writing code with her young husband.

About a week after I had left, I received a WhatsApp message from Manoj.

"Thank you for making the right choice, Vladi-ji. I have a lot to learn from Shalini."

Manoj didn't have to study for long. A year later, he has become Shalini's successor, calmly and wisely managing our new old development centre in Bangalore.

I am happy to say that a colony of monkeys living in my apartment complex has been successfully transported into the wild, after a few failed attempts. The "Primates" have found a new home there, so my ex-neighbours can now keep their fridges unlocked throughout the day.

As for Shalini, we are working together again, this time as transformation consultants. Shalini is in India, and I, I am once again spread around the globe like an electron in orbit, with the highest probability of being in Eastern Europe. India has let me go, but I often fly there for work... when the coronavirus allows me to.

Consulting requires the courage of desperation. Most organizations do well until they need a pathologist for a post-mortem instead of a consultant. Besides, our potential clients — top IT managers — know by themselves what and how to do. Due to their prior experience of transformation, they have become top managers. So they do not need our "advice."

And we don't advise. Our job is to make their dreams come true — we help top managers build a bridge between sweet PowerPoint dreams and harsh corporate reality.

Whether I'm in New York, London, Moscow, or onboard LH754, I'm always happy to talk about radical software rejuvenation, flows, and structures. And about the wise Lord Ganesha, the god of learning, the patron of writers, and other travellers to the physical and virtual worlds.

As much as I'd like to stay with this book, I have to go — this is the last and final call to board a flight on the orchid-powered boat.

www.ingramcontent.com/pod-product-compliance
Lightning Source LLC
LaVergne TN
LVHW051437050326
832903LV00030BD/3125